How to Ski

by MARGARET BENNETT

DRAWINGS BY *Betty Fraser*

SIMON AND SCHUSTER | NEW YORK

Just a Little Bit

The publishers wish to thank the following for permission to reprint material in this book. Any inadvertent omission will be corrected in future printings if notification is sent to the publisher.

Bantam Books, Inc., for a selection from *Bob Beattie's Learn to Ski* by Bob Beattie and Curtis Casewit, copyright © 1967 by Bantam Books, Inc.

Jean Mayer, as quoted by James Egan in "The Passionate Skier," *Saturday Review*, December 27, 1969.

Meredith Press for a selection from *Onassis* by Willi Frischauer, copyright © 1969 by Meredith Press.

New Directions Publishing Corp. for a selection from *Collected Poems* by Dylan Thomas, copyright 1953 by Dylan Thomas.

W. W. Norton, Inc., for a selection from *Last Year at Sugarbush* by Irene Kampen, copyright © 1965 by Irene Kampen.

Charles Scribner's Sons for a selection from *A Moveable Feast* by Ernest Hemingway, copyright © 1964 by Ernest Hemingway, Ltd.

Skiing for a selection from "If You Can Ski, You Can Walk" by Footes Ströller as told to Margaret Bennett, *Skiing*, November 1968.

Universal Publishing and Distributing Corporation for a selection from *A Ski Guide to Europe: The Fabulous Forty* by Abby Rand, copyright © 1968 by Award House.

Published by Simon and Schuster
Rockefeller Center, 630 Fifth Avenue
New York, New York 10020

Second Printing

SBN 671-20683-4
Library of Congress Catalog Card Number: 73-130465
Designed by Irving Perkins
Manufactured in the United States of America
By Mahony & Roese, Inc.

To Lloe, Art, Janis, Chuck, Bob,
Herb, Shar, Barry, Gunther, Bernard,
Franz, Mary Claire, and Anselm,
who made me the skier that I am today
. . . but I forgive them.

Contents

Foreword
and Forewarning

This book is for my soul brothers and sisters—the cowardly and the uncoordinated; the slothful and the self-conscious; the out-of-condition and the inhibited. This book is for those of you who are certain you have absolutely no business on skis, but who desperately want to try. And this book is for those of you who desperately *don't* want to try, but somebody else—husband, wife, friend—is pressuring you onto skis against your will and better judgment. In short, this book is for all of you who can find true happiness on the slopes by skiing not well, but wisely, by skiing not expertly, but just a little bit.

How to Ski
Just a Little Bit

Just a Little Bit

IF YOU'RE SO SMART, HOW COME YOU'RE NOT NANCY GREENE?

Just what, you might ask, are my qualifications for giving advice on skiing? Am I an Olympic champion or a World Cup winner? Did I put a new time in the record book for the Arlberg-Kandahar women's slalom? Well, no. I've

15

never entered any ski competitions other than those desperate life-and-death races that take place on the flat when you're trying to beat someone to the lift line. But I'm certain that if I ever did enter the Arlberg-Kandahar, whatever time I made *would* be a new record, because I'd have no trouble at all taking over three hours to complete the course, though the usual time is around forty-five seconds.

Am I a successful coach and trainer of championship teams or am I a director of one of the country's top ski schools? No, you couldn't call me that, either, although I have in my time shown a number of friends how to fasten their bindings—if they happened to have the same kind of bindings I have—and how to hold their poles and how to sidestep up a small hump in the snow and descend it in a snowplow of glacierlike speed. Also, on one occasion I remember demonstrating the kickturn, managing in the process to whack a lump the size of a crab apple into my shinbone.

Well, then, am I just a fabulous recreational skier who's been at it for years and knows how to handle blindfolded any mountain ever snowed on? No, that's not true, either. Though I sometimes look as if I'm skiing blindfolded, I keep my eyes wide open on the slopes, unless I'm at the top of a hill that's just too horrible to look down. And as for length of time on skis, it's only been three years now, and I started at what the French call *un certain âge*, which means at an age when women no longer tell their age. Objectively analyzing my skills on skis, I would call myself on my best days a weak intermediate and on my worst days a strong beginner.

What then *are* my qualifications to write about skiing? I think you might say my outstanding qualification is my lack of the above qualifications. After all, what superbly muscled and coordinated Olympic gold medalist could tell you how it feels to take up a new and strenuous sport when you're totally out of shape and lacking in any natural athletic ability? What coach of champions knows how humiliating it is to fall off the baby lift or could empathize with that icy ball of fear that forms in your stomach as you tremble at the top of a hill the size of a gopher mound? And what skier who has spent his life on the boards could relate to the problems of someone entering the Martian-strange world of skiing without the mental and physical flexibility of childhood?

All of these traumatizing first ventures into skiing are my specialty—because I've been there. The whole picture is, in fact, indelibly etched on my mind and body. And since my skiing is such a newborn thing, its birth pangs are still so vivid to me that I can describe every muscle contraction.

THERE ARE NO ATHEISTS ON CHAIRLIFTS

Any questions you may ask me about my qualifications, though, are nothing compared to the big question I keep asking myself. Why, I wonder, do I have an overpowering desire to write a book to help more people take up skiing? I own no stock in a ski-equipment company nor yet a piece of the action in any resort. And, besides that, why, when the crowds waiting in the lift lines are already beginning to look like World War II nylon stocking and cigarette queues, should I urge more people onto the already packed—in every sense of the word—slopes, and what's worse, urge them onto my own domain, the easy runs?

The answer is obvious. I'm writing because I can't help myself. Telling me to stop trying to get more people to take up skiing would be like telling a dedicated missionary to knock off converting all those damned heathens because he's going to ruin paradise with crowds.

Skiing *is* like a religion to all of us True Believers, and often, as in religion, the later in life the conversion comes and the more scoffing the original disbelief, the greater the fanaticism of the convert. So no matter how you may doubt now, I swear to you that once you begin skiing, you, too, will become a militant members of the Salvation Army of the slopes. *You* won't be able to help *yourself*, either.

IT'S THE LITTLE BIT YOU SKI THAT COUNTS

Just as to get the most out of religion you don't have to be God, to get the most out of skiing you don't have to be Stein Eriksen. By the way, have you heard the classic Stein-God joke? A skier died and went to heaven—naturally, to a skier heaven is just one big perfect ski mountain covered with snow—and he saw all the late greats of the sport like Buddy Werner and Hannes Schneider schussing around having a marvelous time. Then suddenly Stein, red-gold hair glistening in the sun, skied into view. Surprised, the skier asked St. Peter, "Isn't that Stein Eriksen? I didn't know he'd died." "Oh, that's not Stein Eriksen," said St. Peter. "That's God. He just *thinks* he's Stein Eriksen."

No, to experience all the best that skiing has to offer, just a little bit is all you really need to ski. But you *do* have to ski that little bit. The difference between skiing just a little bit and not skiing at all is vast. It's rather like being just a little bit pregnant and not being pregnant at all.

Many misguided souls feel that they can taste the joys of skiing by going to a ski resort and partaking of the before and after ski with none of the middle. Some, I understand, even pull the old broken-leg bit to lend dignity to their nonparticipation. I don't know how many times I've heard, "Oh, I'll just go along for the trip and watch the rest of you ski and take pictures or something. Don't worry, I won't be bored or get in the way." Don't worry, they always *were* bored and they *did* get in the way.

A non-skiing ski trip just doesn't work, because in most ski resorts—especially in most American ski resorts—no matter what the advertising says, the truth is that there is practically nothing to do during the day except ski. Your only deck companions will be the injured skiers who are so despondent at not being up on the slopes that they are depressing to talk to, if they'll break the sullen barrier long enough *to* talk. The friends or family members with whom you made the trip you see only briefly, as they dash in for a gulp of sustenance for the next run, and if they do sit there with you for a few minutes just to be kind or polite, you can almost see them twitching to be off and skiing. Not at all conducive to a pleasant exchange.

Even during the after-ski time when you expect to do your major swinging you still feel bored and left out. You can't join in the evening's conversation on how great or lousy the snow was, how great or lousy certain runs were, how great or lousy your instructor was or—most popular topic of all—how great or lousy *you* were.

No, if you're the non-skier on a ski trip, you wind up being the locker-key toter or the sweater bringer or the sock washer and in general a menial and peripheral person. You begin to feel like the restroom attendant at an orgy. You grow to hate all those wild-eyed hyperecstatic types stomping around in ski boots, and by the time the trip is over they don't think much of you, either. If they're even slightly sensitive, it's going to be obvious to them that you're having a rotten time and it's going to tone down their fun, and, believe me, they're going to resent it.

But, ah, if you ski *just a little bit*, the whole scene is different. Your days are full and fascinating and fun. At night your muscles are pleasantly tired. You glow with a high-altitude tan. You've earned your *glühwein* ration. You've got tales to tell. You're part of the crowd. You're in. Even if you've spent the entire day snowplowing the nursery slope, you're a skier.

ACCENTUATE THE NEGATIVE

I know that one of the greatest barriers to taking up skiing is that anyone who doesn't ski—whether he wants to or not —usually has a long list of very sound, logical reasons why he shouldn't. I think, therefore, it might be a good idea for us to consider these well-exposed negatives one by one and see if we can develop them into a more positive picture of the sport.

It's Too Dangerous

I won't skirt this issue. I, too, have heard those grim fairy tales of ski poles in the jugular vein—and more un-

mentionable areas; the legends of bashing head-on into ski-lift support towers; the fables of being buried in an avalanche and only being discovered because of a thumb sticking out above the surface—or of not being discovered at all. A particularly juicy part of avalanche lore is the fact that, once under, you can't tell which way is up. Consequently you may start trying to dig yourself out in the wrong direction, which is impractical unless you speak Chinese.

To tell the absolute truth about the hazards of skiing, I acknowledge that there are dozens of ways you can get yours on or near the slopes. Or, at least, there are twenty-six ways, as you can read on the following snow-covered tombstones.

SCHUSSBOOMERS' EPITAPHS
from A to Z

A is for Arthur, who skied through a tree,
B is for Betty, who sat on the T.

C is for Charlie, who thought he was Stein,
D is for Dave, who crashed the lift line.

E is for Edgar, whose goggles got frosted,
F is for Franz, by bunnies exhausted.

G is for Glenn, who was avalanche-buried,
H is for Helen, whose instructor got married.

I is for Ike, sno-cat flat on the hill,
J is for Jock, who saw his lodge bill.

K is for Karen, who was sauna-cooked done,
L is for Lyle, who took "one last run."

M is for Mort, whose wife hated sports,
N is for Ned, who believed snow reports.

O is for Olive, stretch pants squeezed her in two,
P is for Paul, who fell in the fondue.

Q is for Quentin, marooned on a chair,
R is for Roy, who yelled "track" at a bear.

S is for Sue, who flew off a mogul,
T is for Tony, who choked on a yodel.

U is for Una, bored to death in July,
V is for Vincent, whose *bota* ran dry.

W is for Walter, who missed the first turn,
X is for Xena, who stemmed on her stern.

Y is for Yetta, whose bindings released,
Z is for Zeke, whose did not . . .

REST IN PEACE

Yes, skiing *is* dangerous. I won't deny it. But I also want to assure you that ski horror stories are often exaggerated and embellished. Skiers are a lot like fishermen in this respect, and their tales frequently make it sound as if each trip up a T-bar is a miracle of survival—which, of course, in the beginning stages it often really is.

But recreational skiing, seen in the perspective of the modern world, is neither more nor less hazardous than hundreds of everyday activities like taking a bath or crossing a street or eating home-canned green beans. After all, it's dangerous to even breathe these days, city air being what it is, and at least while you're skiing up in the clear pine atmosphere, you're avoiding lung disintegration. Perhaps the best way I can sum up for you my attitude toward the dangers of skiing is to relate a sad story. It happened to the son of a friend of a friend, and I assure you it's absolutely true.

This young man, a passionate skier, decided that before settling down into the conventional mire of Doing What Is Expected, he would fulfill a lifelong dream. The dream was to ski around the world, hitting each major resort on a kind of endless winter odyssey. He worked hard for a year and saved his money and then set off for Switzerland, his first stop. He had been gone less than a week when his parents received a phone call from the American consul telling them that their son was dead. And how did it happen? Did a gondola cable snap? No. Was he impaled on a runaway ski? No. Did he fall into a crevasse lined with jagged rock? No. What happened was that one morning at breakfast in his hotel he choked on a roll.

I'm Too Old to Begin

This negative is uttered, strangely enough, by people of all ages over ten. There is a theory going around that unless your daddy scooped you out of the crib, strapped you onto the boards and hurled you off a mountain before you could walk, the way Stein's and Jean-Claude's daddies did, there's no hope for you as a skier. True, there's probably no hope for you as an Olympic gold-medalist ski champion, but everything else is in the realm of possibility, and most especially is skiing just a little bit.

Listen to this appropriately heartwarming quote from Dr. Merritt H. Stiles, a well-known Spokane, Washington, cardiologist and former vice-president of the American Heart Association. "After having led a relatively sedentary life up to the mid-50's, I took my first lesson in skiing, and during the past few years I have skied actively much of the winter, and have run from two to four miles daily several days each week during the summer to keep in shape, with the result that at 65 I am in infinitely better health than I was at 55."

An Austrian instructor once told me he has much better success with mature beginners than with younger ones. He said older people are much more patient and will learn each step thoroughly before moving on to the next, while the kids are so anxious to rocket down the perpendiculars that they push on too fast, and snap, crackle, pop of bones is sometimes the result. And there is more than just hearsay evidence to support the idea that mature people are less accident-prone. One of the conclusions reached by a study of ski accidents made by the U.S. Army in Germany was that a ski injury is most likely to happen to a person *under twenty years of age.*

Just figure that the older you are the safer and sounder you'll probably be on the slopes. And even if you're in your mid-eighties, if you can still creak and totter around, you can still ski. To paraphrase Browning:

> Grow old along with me
> The best is yet to ski.

It Costs Too Much

Yes, it does, bless it. That's one of the most endearing aspects of skiing. Even in Bob Beattie's quite serious book, *Learn to Ski*, he lists as one of his twelve basic reasons why people decide to ski, "They like to buy equipment (the shopping instinct)," an instinct which in most of us comes on as strong as hunger, thirst, and sex.

What does the high cost of skiing mean? It means that any money you spend on skiing and all its expensive paraphernalia also purchases you a healthy chunk of that most vital commodity, status. Short of owning a string of polo ponies or a yacht, *nothing* gives you more status than skiing. This is mainly because, short of owning a string of polo ponies or a yacht, nothing costs more than skiing. Just think, for example, how many more water-cooler points you get from a mention of your week at Sun Valley than you get from an announcement that you broke 200 at the bowling alley.

I know there are myriads of books and articles that tell you how skiing can be done very inexpensively—on a bootlace, if you will. And, of course, it can. You *can* ski in blue jeans sprayed with Scotchgard and an old sweatshirt filched from a college gym class. You *can* beg, borrow or steal your equipment (the latter, alas, is becoming an increasingly popular method of supply; lock your skis, don't let a teen-ager go wrong). You *can* sleep in the back seat of your car and eat catsup dissolved in hot water with crackers crumbled into it for free in the cafeteria. But if you do that, you're a ski bum. And the sad fact is that if you're a ski bum, you can't be a bum skier. Ski bums all ski more than a little bit. The bummier they are, the better they have to ski. Otherwise they'd have no salve with which to massage their egos.

I think a good rule is that you should spend money on skiing in inverse proportion to your ability. The poorer you are as a skier, the more luxurious should be your accommodations, the more impeccable should be your attire, and, short of buying racing boots and championship skis, which would be a positive handicap, the better should be your equipment. That way you'll have some salve with which to massage *your* ego.

I'm No Athlete

It would be stupid not to admit that anyone in prime physical condition—as athletes *ipso facto* are—has a head start on anyone who is out of shape. However, aside from this, *not* being athletic can sometimes be an advantage. At Mammoth Mountain, California, in the first beginner class I ever took, there was a linesman for a local semipro football team. He was an Orange County Rhino, and he looked it! At about three hundred pounds and 5 feet 9 inches, he was built like a heavy-duty road grader. Earlier in the day, all confident that such a perfect physical specimen would have no trouble taking on any slope without benefit of instruction, he had ridden the gondola to the top of the mountain and hurled himself down. After demonstrating the domino theory with a number of hapless skiers, he was collared by the ski patrol and told it was either a lesson or the showers.

Thus it came to pass that he was mucking around in Guss's Meadow with all of us slack-sinewed stumblebums. And he turned out to be, as the horse-race people might put it, the worst of a poor field. The main reason for his ineptitude was that he was trying to muscle himself through the turns, which doesn't work, since skiing is based more on physics than on the physical. Skiing is also such a beautifully unnatural sport that everything your instincts tell you to do—pull back, lean toward the security of the hill, etc.—will mess you up as a skier. Therefore, your past success in another sport stored in your kinesthetic memory is not necessarily a passkey to skiing proficiency. A competition figure skater I know who specialized in mixed doubles, or whatever they call it, told me her skating partner introduced her to the joys of skiing by taking her to the top of the lift, pointing her downhill and saying, "OK, now just do everything exactly the opposite of what you do when you ice-skate."

Another problem that athletic types sometimes have is one of ego. My husband, Tom, who never was thought of as being particularly athletic either by himself or by his friends, took an old college buddy skiing for the first time last year. Said buddy lettered in high-school football and college water polo and feels in his heart that but for the lack of grace of God his fame on the tennis court would have overshadowed that of Pancho Gonzales. Now, over the previous two years, with luck and pluck and patience and an infinite number of lessons, Tom had worked him-self into a fair stem-christie skier who could handle most of the runs in the not-too-challenging area they were skiing in.

The friend, whose attitude toward Tom has always been, "Any sport you can do I can do ten times better," refused to take lesson one. He also refused to even experiment at the bottom of the hill, side-stepping up and letting Tom show him the basics. "I don't want to waste my time down here, Tom," he said. "Let's just go up on the chair lift. It's OK. I can take care of myself." Nothing could dissuade him. Result: a painfully twisted knee and a mouthful of sour grapes every time the topic of skiing is mentioned to him.

One more point to remember about skiing is that size, or rather lack of it, is no handicap. The good-big-man-is-always-better-than-the-good-little-man theory definitely doesn't hold here. This is one sport in which the ninety-seven-pound weakling can scrape the sand out of his eyes and do as well as Charles Atlas. Some of the top competi-tive skiers—Jean-Claude Killy, Anderl Molterer, Annie Famose, and Nancy Greene, just to give a few examples—tend to be smaller than average, rather than larger. The only advantage a bigger, heavier person has in skiing is that he tends to build up momentum faster, and believe me, those of us who ski just a little bit don't consider *that* an advantage.

Actually, for skiing success it is far better to be a good dancer than to be a good athlete. Rhythm, agility, and technique count for more than muscle power. If they put Nureyev and Joe Namath on skis for the first time, my money would be on Nureyev. After all, I beat an Orange County Rhino and I'm no Fonteyn.

It Takes Too Much Time

Oh, boy, does it! I have an iceberg theory about skiing. That is to say, the time actually spent on skis and skiing represents a vast number of hours beneath the surface that have been spent shopping for clothes and equipment, getting to the resort, dressing and fiddling with equipment, waiting in lines, riding lifts, and pulling yourself up out of the snow after falls. (This last can take a stunning amount of time, especially in the early stages.) But, unlike icebergs, which are only two-thirds invisible, the invisible time in skiing is more like four-fifths or even nine-tenths.

Is this bad? I think not. It merely means that each moment you are skiing is all the more precious because you have had to put in so much time and effort to attain it. A fleeting moment in the elusive arms of skiing is a hundred times more exciting and rewarding than untold hours of wanton wallowing in one of the easy-to-come-by sports.

A New York psychologist who has for many years iceberged the six-to-eight-hour drive to Vermont from New York City claims that skiing wouldn't be the same if you could just take out a couple of hours and run over to Central Park and do it. "The sacrifice, the effort, these are the things that glamorize skiing even more."

The only problem with time consumed in skiing is that it goes by so fast. No matter how long you spend at it, you're so thoroughly absorbed that the hours tick by like so many seconds. Consequently, if you're like that character in *Catch-22* who involved himself only in odious and dull activities so that time would drag and his life would seem to last longer, then avoid skiing. It is such an exhilarating pleasure that it will make your allotted life span seem to have been cut in half.

But I'm Scared

Isn't everyone? Isn't every rational human being scared out of his skull by manifold skiing fears: fear of heights, fear of speed, fear of the caprices of the weather, fear of other skiers, fear of looking like a damned fool, and, worst of all, fear of the unknown?

But even this seemingly insurmountable psychic liability can be analyzed into an actual mental-health advantage. Freud said that we all have basic feelings of helplessness and inadequacy which were hammered—or caressed—into us as infants. And psychologists tell us that one way we can kick these feelings is, as adults, to go out and try to do something "challenging." (Translation: something that scares us out of our skulls.)

And, wow, when you *do* master your ingrained sense of inadequacy and fear on the slopes even for a few moments —which is all you can hope for—there's absolutely nothing like it. A pure, buoyant, revitalizing wave of omnipotence, a sensation of being bigger than life, sweeps over you. This is a feeling that's mighty hard to come by these days in a society that seems designed to make us all feel like automated pygmies—and, therefore, one that's worth going through a good bit of trouble and terror to experience.

But even when you are in what I consider to be the normal skiing state—that is, gelatinous intestines clamped tight around lily liver—there's something positive to be said for that, as well. The person who first explained this to me was a British gentleman with whom I shared the nightly dinner table in Saalbach. He was the vigorous, florid-faced pukka sahib sort, who in an earlier era no doubt would have spurted his adrenalin in colonial skirmishes rather than on the slopes of Austria. "Ski holidays are the only kind I take now," he told me. "Skiing's the one thing that can really take my mind off my business worries. When I'm up there on the mountain, I'm so bloody frightened I can't think of anything except survival."

I Just Know I Can't Do It

Oh, yes you can—although if you have any serious doubts that skiing might be detrimental to your health, you should consult a doctor (preferably a doctor who skis). In general, you can't find the word "can't" in the skiing lexicon. Take Dr. Albert Rosen, for whom the horrendously steep Al's Run at Taos is named. He has a heart condition that makes it necessary for him to ski with a tank of oxygen strapped to his back for emergencies. Take the many amputees who ski on one ski and find skiing superb mental as well as physical therapy. Take the blind skiers. Yes, I said *blind.* And if you still have the audacity to cry "can't," take Herr Hoodwinks Holiday Schmaltz. Schmaltzie skis and Schmaltzie is a dog. Not some big-brute-type dog, either, but a mild-mannered long-haired Dachshund. He was always so despondent when his owners, the Dr. H. Clagett Harding family of Portland, Oregon, left him at home when they went on ski trips that they finally broke down and fitted him up with special skis. Now he goes everywhere with them, including, just last year, Austria. If they ever organize dog Olympics, Schmaltzie is ready to bring home three gold medals, and the Hardings are bringing up his son and daughter, Sitzmark von Schmaltz and Schönes Wurstchen, to follow in his ski tracks. *You* can't ski? Bah, humbug!

PROOF POSITIVE

I don't, however, urge you to take up skiing simply because it is not so bad, but rather because it *is* so good. For example:

Skiing Is Sexy

I hate to sound like Helen Gurley Brown, who is forever making sappy lists of sexy things: "Being able to sit very still is sexy"; "Liking men is sexy"; "Clean hair is sexy." Still, I can't help saying it: Skiing *is* sexy. There's no getting around the fact. It's sexy literally and figuratively, directly and indirectly.

As Taos chief instructor Jean Meyer says, "In my teaching I emphasize feelings, sensation. It becomes something almost sensual. . . . It's a lust, a joy. . . It's ebullience, exuberance. You're happy, you're in love." And all this frigid passion takes place on what the director, Ernie Blake, calls "the world's sexiest powder."

Psychologist Carolyn Schreiber puts it on the hot line more clinically: "There's a sexual aspect to skiing. It has to do with the speed—the exhilaration of gliding over the snow; that rare feeling when you're almost out of control. There's a loss of one's self, one's ego boundary, as in an orgasm." And the lovely part of skiing is that you can do it *alone*.

Mind you, I'm not advocating skiing as a substitute for

sex, although there are a lot worse ways to sublimate. I'm just saying that this sexual aspect is part, albeit a sub-conscious part, of skiing's irresistible attraction.

But that's not all. To Helen-Gurley-Brown it even fur-ther: stretch pants are sexy, turtlenecks are sexy, sitting knee-to-knee in a gondola is sexy, roaring fires in ski chalets are sexy and fur rugs in front of these roaring fires are sexy, and to top it off, here's one of Miss Brown's own sexies that I agree with totally—good health is sexy. The fatal appeal of tubercular types like Camille and Chopin notwithstanding, any red-blooded male or female of the species will be more naturally drawn to someone who glows and vibrates with vitality than to members of the flaccid, hollow-chested, green-tinged-pallor set. And skiing can give you that glow and those vibrations, because . . .

Skiing Is Healthy

It goes without saying that all that clear air and sunshine have to be good for captives of our sedentary society, so I won't say it. Another thing that goes without saying is that you shouldn't overdo it on the if-one-aspirin-makes-me-feel-good-I'll-take-the-whole-bottle theory. But this is one thing that goes without saying that can't be said too often, so I'll say it again: Don't overdo; don't indulge in too much of a good thing.

Here is where the advantages of skiing just a little bit come into full play. The trick, and I admit it's not the easiest one to perform, is getting enough exercise to pre-vent a heart attack, and yet not enough to bring one on; to ski in a way that strengthens your limbs without snapping them. But more about how to perform that particular sleight-of-ski later. For now, believe me when I say skiing just a little bit makes you feel marvelous and in the process makes you look marvelous, which brings us to another positive proof.

Skiing Is a Beauty Treatment

Aspenglow or Cortina luminescence or whatever the brochure writers want to call it, you do come away from skiing with an aura about you. It's only partially the high-altitude tan, which is incidentally quite different from the seashore or backyard variety, more alive and less dried out, somehow. The other part of your aura comes from all that blood galloping around in your veins and arteries and capillaries. The toning up of the muscles helps, too, as does the redistribution of weight that invariably occurs, making it possible for you to buy ski pants at the beginning of the season a size too small in the waist and find they fit at the end of your first week-long ski trip.

I also think a big part of the good-looks angle of skiing comes with the clothes you wear. Ski clothes, both the during and after variety, are in my opinion the best-looking, best-designed and most flattering sports attire on the market. I've often argued that anybody short of Mama Cass and Jackie Gleason looks fabulous in ski clothes, because they scrunch and squeeze you into shape and cover up a number of corporeal sins. Those with whom I've argued this point maintain that ski clothes, at least the stretch pants, show up every flaw. I will agree to this extent:

> With a Rubens rear or a Falstaff pot,
> In stretch pants you won't look so hot.

Otherwise, if you're even just fair to middling in the quality of your physique, ski clothes are guaranteed to make you look better than you really are. And if you *do* have the Rubens rear or the Falstaff pot, jump suits are very in this season.

Skiing Is Companionable

OK, now, so you're sexy and you look good and you feel good. What happens next with you and skiing? You interact with other skiers. And they're people well worth interacting with, with the exception of a few yahoos. (The one time in my life I've ever received an obscene phone call was when I was staying at a grotesquely expensive lodge at Snowmass. I console myself with the thought that it must have been a snowmobile driver.) To attract advertisers to their publication *Ski Magazine* runs full-page ads describing how superb skiers are as a group, and it makes them all sound like direct descendants of the Medicis. And that's not far from the truth. Look at some of the people who are enthusiastic skiers. In politics, you find all the Kennedys and Galbraith (of the latter it has been said he skis with great dignity, looking something like de Gaulle descending on an escalator) and McNamara and Romney and Udall and Lindsay and Buckley. If your admiration is focused on the entertainment world, you could come up, just for starters, with Eddie Albert and Janet Leigh and Andy Williams and Kim Novak and Jim Arness and Jean Seberg and Efrem Zimbalist and Natalie Wood and Robert Redford and Petula Clark and Audrey Hepburn and Leonard Bernstein. Even the Burtons have a home in Gstaad, although I can't guarantee that they let skiing intrude excessively on their more publicized activities.

Some say that skiers are snobs, and it's true. They are terrible snobs, but not with each other. They are only snobbish toward people who don't ski, and why not? They have every right to feel superior to those who haven't had their baptism of snow.

Here again that vast difference between skiing just a little bit and not skiing at all raises its hoary head. Riding up on a lift, your companion asks no credentials other than those fastened onto your boots. The chairman of the board and the office boy have a perfect meeting of the mind and spirit. It also doesn't matter if you're riding up for a rocket trip down the experts' chute or if your destination is a careful picking of your way down the bunny bowl. Whatever be your route and method of descent, you're still another skier and worthy of attention and conversation.

It is this clubby, open friendliness that makes skiing such a great get-acquainted sport for the available of both sexes. This is especially true for members of that vast majority-minority group, the unmarried girls. Now hear this. The ratio of men to women in ski resorts is at its very worst 3 to 2, and at its best it approaches the numerical advantages for a girl of being a stowaway on an aircraft carrier.

Should some permanent liaison be negotiated from a brief encounter at a ski resort, the prognosis for success is extremely good. The advantage of husband-and-wife and family skiing has become a truism of togetherness simply because it *is* true. And the reverse is equally true. Margaret Mead, our friendly neighborhood expert on marriage, once said in a speech in San Francisco that she holds out small hope for a union in which one partner skis and the other doesn't.

This marital rule holds on all levels of society. Just as the Colonel's Lady and Judy O'Grady are sisters under the stretch pants, so are the shipping clerk and the shipping magnate brothers. Think, for example, how the gossip-column history of the world would have been changed had Aristotle Onassis learned how to ski. Onassis' biographer, Willi Frischauer, attributes the break-up of his first marriage partially to his lack of interest and ability in skiing. At least, that's the impression you get, since he brings it up so frequently with such quotes as:

... it was not easy to put one's finger on the trouble. Was it that Tina found too much enjoyment in her winter sports excursions in which Ari rarely shared? ... A skiing excursion with a young beau while Ari was not about ... Tina loved winter sports ... Onassis, himself, was no skiing enthusiast. "When I went skiing," he said, "it was mainly on my backside."

On a macabre note, there was recently a Los Angeles murder-suicide case in which a wealthy contractor was shot by his former fiancée because he was forsaking her and marrying another girl whom he had met—where else? —on a ski trip.

But to continue in more of a life-can-be-beautiful tone, the Aga Khan was first introduced to his now wife, Lady Crichton-Stuart, while he was on a ski holiday in St. Moritz. The old white magic works for us serfs, too. On a charter flight to Europe I met a couple in their 50s. The wife, a tanned wiry little type who radiated personality and vitality, told me that her husband refused to marry her until she learned how to ski. "That was back in the days before they had many lifts," she said with a nostalgic grimace, "so, since I spent more time climbing up the hill than skiing down, it took me two years, but I learned." And from the companionable bone-crushing arm-around-the-shoulder hugs her husband frequently gave her, her efforts were appreciated and they were skiing happily ever after.

Skiing is just as companionable down on the flatland as it is up in the mountains. Skiers are as irresistibly drawn to each other at social gatherings as alcoholics are to the gin bottle. Al Greenberg, executive editor of *Skiing Magazine*, says it's always amazing to him that when he attends parties that include some of the really important people in government and the arts, where you'd expect the conversation to bounce from foreign policy to existentialism to the space program to *cinéma verité*, what does everyone want to talk about? You guessed it. Skiing. And he says from personal experience that "those who have some expertise in ski matters are social lions ranking in demand somewhere between the matinee idol and the rock-and-roll guitarist."

I've also found it true that at a cocktail or dinner party when I find myself isolated with someone with whom it appears I have zilch in common and the conversation is dying of slow strangulation, if by lucky happenstance we reveal to each other that we're skiers, we're off and running with endless conversational material and we suddenly find each other fascinating.

The bond between skiers does you good in all kinds of unexpected places. For instance, I know an avid-rabid skier who is a college librarian to support the habit. She tells me that when she finds out a student requesting help is a fellow addict, he gets as much attention as if he were the president of the college—or maybe a little more.

Skiing Is Solitary

Isn't this a direct contradiction of the companionship bit? Not at all. The actual act of skiing has to be done alone. Skiing is solitude, but solitude in the best sense of the word. It is not loneliness-solitude, but self-fulfilling solitude. Instead of feeling lost in the crowd as you do in the city, you feel you have at last found yourself in the isolation of the slopes. Of course, if you can only ski on weekends and school holidays, this aloneness on the slopes has to be a state of mind rather than an actuality.

This sensation of being at one with yourself is one of the most revitalizing aspects of skiing. I have a non-skiing friend who has a skiing husband. Every once in a while he insists on escaping the pressures of business by heading for the slopes. He goes alone. All day long he skis the wax off his heads—alone. He wolfs down dinner alone and he drops exhausted into bed—still alone. Since he always returns home looking as fresh and new as if he just rolled off the assembly line at the man factory, his wife strongly suspects that he spends his time in the mountains engaging in hanky-panky-going-on-orgy. This only points up her ignorance of the aftereffects of both skiing and orgies.

At any rate, going skiing is the best way there is to get acquainted with that aloof stranger, yourself. Who knows, you may find, especially after you meet some particularly challenging challenge, that you like yourself a lot better than you ever dreamed you could or would.

Skiing Is Beautiful

For a lifelong city dweller like me it's hard not to get sloppy and trite when talking about the beauties of nature a skier is privileged to observe through the Baccarat-clear air of the mountains—the trees with their white wool winter coats, the bowls of untracked whipped cream, the peaks punching holes in the mist to stick their heads in the sun. All this is the personal property of the skier. Some non-skiers think they can get the same sights and sensations by just riding to the top of the gondola, looking around and saying, "Nice view there," and riding back down again. Not so. It doesn't work. This is because you're only *observing* nature from the outside; you're not an actual interacting part of it the way you are when you ski. Also, some of the most magnificent moments of natural beauty are not necessarily available to those standing around at the top of the lift. These are the moments that come upon you unexpectedly in the volatile atmosphere of the mountains. You round a bend and suddenly, *pow*, all the elements—sky, trees, clouds, mountains, snow, sun—implode into a blast of beauty that almost knocks you off your skis.

Then, too, there's the heightening of perception that occurs after you've been terrorized by a run. Never does the world look more glorious to you than in those moments immediately after you thought you were leaving it forever.

All of this belongs to skiers and *only* to skiers, and the knowledge that the earth-creepers down below will never see what you see and, more important, see it in the way that you see it, intensifies the already excruciating loveliness of the mountains.

Skiing Is Transcendental

Look in any dictionary for a definition of the word "transcendental." You'll find such lexicographical gropings as "idealistic"..."individualistic"..."mystical in spirit"... "lying beyond ordinary limits"..."supreme"... "outside consciousness"... "a system holding that there are modes of being outside the reach of mundane experience." All of that is what skiing is—and more. I find it just as difficult to put the transcendental essence of skiing into words as the dictionary does to define "transcendental" itself.

Skiing is an experiencing that transcends ordinary experience. You can't know what it is until you've been through it yourself, and then, grope as you will, you won't be able to spell it out so a non-skier can understand. The wild-eyed babbling attempts of skiers to explain what it's all about are what give non-skiers the impression that all skiers are nuts.

So if you haven't skied, it's impossible for me to explain the transcendentalism of skiing to you, and when you have skied, I won't need to explain it.

Unparalleled Pleasure and How to Get It

I realize that all this rhapsodizing makes skiing sound like a pretentious combination of God, vitamin pills and a Dale Carnegie course, so I'll quickly add that the best part of skiing is that it's just plain fun. It's fun, that is, if you don't try to turn it into work. It's fun, if you stick to skiing just a little bit.

At this point I think I'd better explain exactly what in the Sam Hill and Aspen Mountain this skiing just a little bit that I keep hammering you over the stocking cap with *is*. Does it mean that you only ski a couple of weekends a year? Definitely not. Skiing just a little bit has nothing to do with how many days you ski. Last season I spent a total of six and a half weeks on skis, which I consider above average, and yet, I assure you, I ski just a little bit.

No, skiing just a little bit refers to quality rather than quantity. It has to do with *how* you ski rather than with *how much* you ski. The only way I can explain it is by first defining a few basic ski terms. These terms you need to know are really *turns*. I've often heard ski instructors say that skiing is actually turning, so you can measure your progress up the skiing ladder by the kind of turn you make. We'll start with the lowest rung.

Snowplow

This is the first maneuver you learn on skis, because it's not only a way to turn but also—vitally important at this stage of the sport—a way to stop. What you do is, with your feet apart, make yourself pigeon-toed and press down and out on the inside edges of your skis. This makes your skis push up the snow in front as if they were blades of a—you guessed it—snowplow. If you put all of your weight on the right ski, you turn left, and vice versa.

There is absolutely nothing wrong with the snowplow as a turn except that it's more exhausting than being a stevedore in a steel port and—let's call a snowplow a snowplow—it's ugly and you look and feel like a clod doing it. There is none of the grace and freedom associated with this graceful and free sport. Doing the snowplow is definitely *not* skiing just a little bit. It is, in fact, hardly skiing at all.

But don't despise the poor old snowplow for not really being skiing. Accept it for what it is: something that will give you a feeling of security because you know it's always there to fall back on (rather than something else you might fall back on). It also teaches you the physical principles of skiing and nudges you along toward what you really want to do.

Besides that, it is a basic I think shouldn't be skipped the way they do in the short ski and the *Natur Teknik* schools. I know a really good skier who skipped ladder rung no. 1 but who had to go back and learn it, because at Mammoth Mountain, where he does most of his skiing, to come off chair lift 3 a snowplow is all you have room to do to slow yourself down before you schuss the chute, and if you don't know the snowplow and are loath to bash into your fellow citizens, you are denied some of the loveliest skiing on the mountain.

Stem Turn and Stem Christie

Stemming means moving one ski out from beside the other and pointing it in the direction of your turn. It's a kind of half-a-snowplow. You then bring the other ski up next to it and complete your turn. If you throw in a sliding motion after you bring your skis together, that makes the "christie" part of the stem christie. When you do stem turns and stem-christie turns, you are skiing back and forth across the slope with your skis together (traversing) except when you actually make the turn, so you look good and you feel good. When you turn by stemming, your

turns are relatively easy and safe and pleasant. Hence, in skiing circles stemming is universally despised. I have heard skiers as furiously deny the quite obvious fact that they stem as they would deny an accusation of child molesting.

Parallel

This is the top rung of the ladder. Skiing parallel is what you see people do in movies and travelogues, unless a few shots of my kind are included for comic relief. When you ski parallel it means that your skis are always side by side as you ski—through the turns and everything—preferably touching and clattering hollowly so everybody can *hear* you're skiing parallel, even if you don't happen to be in their line of vision. Your knees and ankles are also glued together. Your track down the mountain looks as if it were made with one ski instead of two. Skiing parallel is the essence of the good and the true and the beautiful in skiing. It is also virtually impossible for a normal human being to do most of the time and it is absolutely impossible for even a superhuman being to do all the time. That, of course, is why everyone on skis is always trying to do it.

Now you are familiar with the basic range of skiing turns and you're prepared to understand what I mean by skiing just a little bit. Listen carefully. I mean learning the snowplow, the stem turn, the stem christie—and then just remaining on that level and forgetting forever to try to learn to ski parallel. This is wild and blatant sacrilege to dyed (and sometimes died)-in-the-wool skiing enthusiasts. It is anathema to professional ski instructors. But to me it is the sole secret of joy on skis.

CONTAGIOUS PARALLELITIS INSIDIUS

But, alas, although forgetting about skiing parallel is the most important piece of advice I can give you, it is probably also going to be the hardest for you to follow. It is easier to forget that smoking is injurious to your health than it is to forget trying to ski parallel, because from the moment your boots touch the boards you will have it unceasingly drummed into your conscious and subconscious that it's the *only* way to ski. In fact, and here's an even more blatant and brazen breaking of the truth in advertising code, you'll be informed that you're not really a skier unless you can ski parallel.

In your first lesson, hardly has your instructor shown you how to hold your poles before you hear, "Of course, what you all want to do is ski parallel, so we'll get through these little preliminaries as quickly as possible...." All the way up through the various class levels it's the same refrain—"Of course, you all want to ski parallel"—until you become as obsessed by it as the instructor.

The worst level of all for this brainwashing is in the stem-christie class. You dutifully stand under the ski-school sign that says "Stem Christie," because you have the idea that you would like to learn or try to perfect that quite lovely and honorable turn that is really all a body needs to know to ski on happily through eternity, and what happens? Your instructor has the class go through a couple of stem christies while he observes you with distaste, as if you were committing an obscene act. Then, no matter how well or poorly the stem christies were executed, he sighs with relief that this odious and disgusting part of the lesson is over and says, "So now you all want to learn to ski parallel, *ja?*" (or some ethnic variation thereof), and like a pack of Pavlov's sled dogs, all members of the class loll their tongues and wag their tails with delight at the prospect.

If you happen to be at a resort where they have beginning and advanced stem-christie classes and you are in the advanced section, the token couple of stem christies are eliminated and you start right in on parallel. It is for this reason that I feel it is impossible ever to learn the advanced stem christie in a class, because they never teach it. Every advanced stem-christie class I've ever been in—and believe me, that's plenty of stem-christie classes—has taught parallel skiing almost exclusively. This leads me to wonder idly what it is they do in the parallel classes. I say idly because I swear on my Ullr medal that I'm never going to get into one and find out, and I urge you to swear the same.

But to continue, once they have infected you with the germ of wanting to ski parallel, you are in a constant fever to do it. All skiing pleasure is denied you because all you can think of is kicking the stemming habit. When you should be wallowing in the pure joy of stem-christieing the slope, you are staring at your ski tips with a fixed frown to see if you can catch one sneaking into the stem (you always can) or you are contracting your stomach muscles and (*umpf!*) trying to heave yourself off the snow to "hop" into your parallel. You end each day feeling worn out and defeated instead of invigorated and elated.

To put it in other terms, you are something like a man who owns a beautiful Mercedes-Benz but can't get any pleasure out of driving it because he's so hung up on moving up to a Rolls-Royce. And this miserable situation can go on for years. As former Olympic coach Bob Beattie states, "It may take only three or four supervised ski sessions to become an intermediate skier, but at least one to two full ski seasons will go by before you can swing down a steep mountain with both skis together. . . . In fact, I've known some enthusiastic skiers who still can't do a parallel christie after ten years and longer."

I'll drink to that. I'll even drink to some of us *never* being able to do it, and why should we try? Why should we turn all the potentially beautiful years of skiing into season after season of nothing but blood, sweat, toil, and tears in quest of what is quite possibly impossible?

By the way, Schmaltzie, the skiing Dachshund, has the good sense to stick to the stem christie.

BORED ON THE BOARDS?

You may wonder if it will be tedious for you to do just one stem christie after another forever. Not at all. In the first place, you won't be doing them all the time. In moments of extreme terror you'll invariably lapse back into the snowplow for security just as even the best of the parallel skiers will automatically, in time of stress, *zap!*, stick out that stem.

In the second place, the term encompasses such an infinite variety of techniques within itself that it still strikes me as impossible for anyone to be bored with stem christies.

If they did one of those evolution charts for skiing of the kind that they do for the history of the earth that shows man's stay as an inch while the rest of the time of the earth's existence is a mile, I think it would work out with the snowplow and parallel turns as inches and the stem christie as a mile. In fact, there's more than a mile between a beginning and an advanced stem christie. On the other hand, a snowplow is a snowplow is a snowplow and there's not much room for variations. And just as a pint's a pound the world around, a true parallel skier and his turns are much the same everywhere, despite minor national variations. These national variations, incidentally, are *quite* minor, as was demonstrated in a recent Interski where representatives of the ski schools of the different skiing countries get together to compare and contrast techniques. On the last demonstration day the instructors, for fun, changed sweaters with each other. Most observers did not know the difference; many were overheard making comments like, "Jeez, you can always tell an Austrian, can't you—look at that angulation and counter-rotation," and it turned out the skier was actually Japanese.

The vast mile-wide level known as "intermediate," though, encompasses absolutely everything that falls between snowplow and parallel. It can be a stem so wide and held so long and executed so slowly that it's indistinguishable from a snowplow except that it starts off and ultimately finishes with the skier in a traverse position. And way over on the other end it can also be a stem christie with such an infinitesimally small stem and with the skis together through the whole turn and at such speed that it looks so much like a parallel christie that you could fake it and say it was and you'd probably never get found out. Only your ski instructor would know for sure. Incidentally, I once read that one of the Austrian founding fathers of skiing used to argue vehemently that there's no such thing as a pure parallel turn. He said that there's *always* a millimeter of stemming taking place, but it's just impossible to see. An interesting theory and one that should give you much solace—I know it does me.

The infinite variety of turns, then, that are included in the stem/stem-christie level to deliver you from boredom is squared by the infinite differences of slopes and of slope conditions. Even if you go down the same slope using the identical turn you used before, but do it ten minutes later, it's a different run entirely. The weather is cooler or it's warmer. The snow is softer or it's harder. Other skiers have rearranged the malleable terrain into a new pattern. Maybe an inch of new powder has dropped. Maybe the panzer division has come by with its scrapers and rollers to shave off the moguls—those bumps in the snow formed by turning skiers. Who knows? The only thing you can know is that the run is going to be new and different. A ski run is like a French housewife's soup continually bubbling on the back burner. Each day new ingredients are thrown in—a few leftover carrots, a half head of cabbage, maybe some mushroom stems. Each time it's served up, it's an original concoction, never tasted before and never to be tasted again. And as a result, the family never says, "Ho-hum, same old soup again, eh, Maman?" They always lap it up with enthusiasm for the delicious surprise that it is.

HOW—AND HOW <u>NOT</u>—TO LEARN TO SKI

A Little Book Learning Is a Dangerous Thing

This now is the logical place to give you step-by-step instructions on how to ski. But logical though it may be, that is exactly what I'm *not* going to do. I'm not going to do it, because I am convinced that it is absolutely and irrevocably impossible to learn how to ski from reading a book. I'm not alone in this belief. As a matter of fact, every author of every how-to-ski book I've ever read states firmly in the opening chapter that you cannot learn how to ski from a book. He then proceeds to spend the rest of the book trying to teach you how to ski.

If it were just a mere matter of its being impossible to teach you how to ski in a book, I would go ahead and try. I always enjoy a challenge. That's one of the reasons I like skiing. The main reason I'm not doing it is that any attempt I might make would be a positive detriment to you. I know this from experience. Every time I've read a book that tells in simple terms the simple steps involved in skiing, I can't ski for two weeks afterward. My head is so full of the multitude of things I ought to be remembering to do that I'm too tangled up in my mind to do anything with my body. I become a mental stumblebum. This is because when even the most basic of physical acts is written up, it becomes a marvel of complexity and confusion, no matter how simple and easy the writer keeps insisting it really is.

In case you doubt me, let me show you how this works. I will here take a very well-known book on skiing and turn it around to see how it would read if it tried to teach you how to do something you do almost without thinking about it.

If You Can Ski, You Can Walk

Some encouraging words for skimeisters, schussboomers, ski bums, and all others who were "born on the boards" and who long to experience the wonderful world of walking.

by Footes Ströller

NOTE: The author, popularly known as "the father of modern walking," is a veteran and pioneer walking instructor. He coached the strike-winning 1967 AFL-CIO picketing team, helped polish the natural walking style of President Harry S Truman, and only last year accomplished the heretofore impossible feat of coaxing Stein Eriksen off his skis and encouraging him to take his first faltering steps. Herr Ströller is also justly famed as the inventor of the Ströller Snap-Away Safety Shoelace, which totally revolutionized the sport of walking.

Admit it. From time to time as you pause in mid-slope in the lengthening shadows of late afternoon and look down at the lodge and see people off their skis casually waddling around the sun deck, you feel a surge of envy. What would it be like, you think, to slip on a pair of soft after-ski boots or hand-sewn loafers and experience such joyous freedom of movement?

Still, you reason sadly, it's too late for you to take up an activity as potentially dangerous (over 100,000 persons per year are seriously injured in walking accidents) and you are embarrassed at the thought of stumbling around at your age while little children whose parents early encouraged them in walking are toddling confidently.

But I guarantee, you need have no fear. If you can ski, you *can* walk. You *can* join the others who pried themselves off their skis and stepped into a new and exhilarating existence.

THE MANY JOYS OF THE WALKER

Just what is the powerful appeal of this seemingly simple sport? Much of walking's attraction lies in the test it provides for man against the forces of nature—the thrill of dodging traffic and agilely skirting open manholes in the city streets, the excitement of crossing a field where bulls are idly grazing, or of strolling along a boulder-strewn path. Yes, walking's succession of challenges and recurrent risks make it qualify as a nerve-tingling survival sport that puts you on your mettle.

Then there's the lure of escaping the crowded slopes and teeming lift lines. It is truly gratifying to elude the mobs of raucous-voiced skiers who jam every resort and to flee to the quiet back streets of the city where the only sounds you hear are the click of your own heels on the pavement and the occasional distant screech of brakes or crash of metal or roar of a motorcycle.

And, frankly, walking has a good deal of snob appeal. Only when you are a walker can you casually strike up a conversation with your chair-lift partner about the amusing thing that happened to you when you last strolled the Via Veneto or the Champs-Elysées or the Ginza. Any time you meet a fellow walker on the slopes or in a lift line, you have an instant bond, something that sets you distinctively apart from the common herd of the snowbound.

Expensive clothing and equipment, too, are an integral part of the charm of the sport. Although in the smaller cities many young people can and do enjoy walking in jeans and tennis shoes, along the more exclusive sidewalks such as Park Avenue and Wilshire Boulevard and North Michigan Avenue, costly tailored suits and handmade English shoes and *haute couture* costumes are *de rigueur* and promenading up and down in them gives the wearer a distinct feeling of affluent superiority.

There is also the companionship inherent in walking that makes the ideal family sport. On the ski slopes the father is usually found up in the more difficult runs; the mother may be trying to break the stemming habit somewhere in the intermediate areas; the teen-age son may be schussing the face; and the smaller children may be engaged in snow play or lessons down on the bunny runs. These family members hardly ever see each other or even exchange a word for days on end; communication is destroyed; and the family unit breaks down. But, as the saying goes, "The family that walks together, talks together." In walking, all members of the family, side by side, can enjoy perfecting their skills on the identical sidewalk or park path.

Many romances, too, have begun as a result of sidewalk "pick-ups."

These reasons, along with other more personal, individual, inexplicable psychological drives—reasons that defy wholly rational explanation—account for the tremendous recent increase of interest in the sport.

A BIT OF HISTORY

Although walking as a sport is a recent development, its origins can be traced to the end of the Ice Age. It was at this time that man's early hominid ancestor, the *Australopithecus*, forced by receding snows to find some method of dry-land locomotion, wrapped his feet in animal skins and took his first hesitant steps. For many centuries after this, walking remained primarily a practical necessity, *e.g.*, skiers would occasionally unfasten their skis and clumsily stumble across the uneven ground to obtain wine or ale, utilize rest rooms, give birth, etc. But then, as so frequently happens, what began as a necessity gradually evolved into a fascinating sport in and of itself, and modern walking was born.

TAKING UP WALKING

At the onset it must be admitted that walking is not a natural act like traversing or sideslipping. There is, in fact, no such thing as a born or intuitive walker. Every movement you must perform in walking goes contrary to a skier's instincts. Then, too, your walking shoes with their thin soles and lack of ankle support will reinforce your feelings of clumsiness and insecurity—and many novice walkers confess they feel in constant jeopardy without their poles to lean upon.

When you first begin walking, then, you must be prepared to find every fiber within you rebelling against the unaccustomed movements. This is because each step you take thrusts your body from a state of balanced equilibrium—such as it enjoys when both feet are planted solidly on skis—into a state of fleeting instability. Only the action of the muscles keeps the walker from falling flat on his face. It has been said, in fact, that the process of walking is nothing more than one controlled fall after another.

If we break down the walking process into simple components, the action is as described by the eminent walking expert Arthur J. Snider, writing in *Science Digest*: "It begins with the body pitching slightly but precariously forward. One leg quickly swings through and makes contact with the ground so that the center of body weight is again safely between the two legs. Then the rear leg starts through, pushing off against the ground, first with the ball of the foot and then the big toe. Before making contact with the ground again, the leg straightens at the knee but remains bent at the ankle. Thus the heel strikes the ground first."

It is only through mastering these motions in conjunction with the basic walking rhythm of down-up-stepping (or, as some walking instructors who favor the Indian technique prefer, up-down-stepping) that the walker can eventually manipulate his feet into a series of linked steps that will give him the maneuverability to perform with skill and confidence in all walking situations, including odd surface conditions such as cobblestones, loose gravel, mud, etc.

Although all this may seem complicated, there is a logical learning progression which can make it possible for any skier regardless of age and athletic ability to learn to walk. Here I cannot emphasize too strongly the importance of taking lessons from a professional instructor. There have been a number of tasteless jokes over the years about the uselessness and expense of walking instructors. I'm sure you've all heard the old rhyme, "Heel and toe/Away you go/Slip me some dough." But I assure you there is far more poetry than truth in this. Walking instructors are for the most part truly dedicated people who love the feel of the sidewalk beneath their feet and who have an almost missionary zeal to help others to experience the pleasurable sensations of walking. They know the latest techniques and shortcuts that can make you an accomplished walker in a single season.

Still skeptical? Still afraid you can't make the transition from snow to sidewalk? Then try this experiment. Stand erect on your skis on a bit of flat snow-covered ground. Now push your left foot forward, lifting it slightly. Bring the ski to a stop, stepping down hard, heel first, bending your knee slightly. Repeat the action with your right foot. See? You automatically shifted your weight from one foot to the other—the basic technique in walking. This means you are ready and able to start your first lesson: walking in shoes over asphalt or cement.

But enough of talk. Now is the time for action. Now is the time for all of you to get down off those mountains, put on shoes, and head for the towns. When you do, you'll be amazed to find how quickly you lose your Heads and your Harts to this enthralling sport—and how wonderful it is at last to discover your soles.

See how it works? Or rather, doesn't work. I've actually heard of actors who, on being told to walk across the stage, were immobilized when they thought about it and started analyzing things like which arm went forward with which foot. I've also heard of similar experiences concerning sex-manual readers, but that's another even longer and sadder story.

If, then, I'm not going to tell you how to ski, what am I going to tell you? I am going to tell you how to *learn* how to ski—in other words, how to go about acquiring the basic skiing skills without either maiming or terrifying yourself any more than absolutely necessary. This takes strategy, strategy as devious and complex as a Clausewitz battle plan.

Low and Dry

There are all kinds of city-located pre-ski learning gimmicks going around these days. There are the dry-land ski lessons that are sometimes a part of high school and college gym classes, in which you stomp and scoot around on straw or some other semi-slippery substance. There are the small slopes located in the parking lots of ski shops. These slopes are covered with some kind of crystal that gives you at least a *remote* sensation of skiing. And there is the ski deck, a motorized rolling, sloping carpet. You stay in one place and the carpet relentlessly moves toward you, as you fight for your balance, if not your life.

Using the first two of these methods, you can learn the basic principles of walking on skis, sidestepping, herringbone, and the snowplow. On the third device, the ski deck, you could conceivably learn anything and probably learn it better than you could on the slopes. In fact, you'd have to learn it better, because the snow often forgives an error, but the ski deck peremptorily slaps you down for it.

Before I went on my first ski trip I signed up for a course

of six lessons on one of these rolling carpets. I only got up to two before I quit in pain and exhaustion. But I'll admit those two lessons helped immeasurably. One of the things they did, in fact, was to get me accustomed to pain and exhaustion, those two handmaidens of beginning skiing. On a more practical level, I also learned how to sidestep up a hill, hanging my body out into space to make the skis bite in, and I learned the snowplow position.

In all of these pre-ski workout systems, besides getting the feel of the equipment and at least getting acquainted with the basics, there are two other very important advantages.

1. You get your muscles so sore you can hardly move *before* you go on your ski trip. This is not a crucial matter if you're only going up to the snow for one day, because you can just come home and writhe and hobble for a few days and nothing is lost. But if you're going on a several-day to week-long excursion, you can blow the whole trip if you get yourself into such a state of muscle agony on the first day that you can't even bend over to fasten your bindings on the second. Dry-land classes and artificial hills can prevent this.

2. By comparison with the boredom of the dry-land classes and the crystal slope and the agony of the rolling ski deck, real skiing is so pleasant and easy and wonderful that you are immediately enchanted and captivated by it and you have a lovely ski trip. This advantage may be related to the old joy of bashing your head on the wall because it feels so good when you stop, but it works, at least for me. A skiing friend who watched me work out on one of my ski-deck lessons went away shaking his head. Later he told me, "I thought that thing would turn you against skiing for life. Believe me, if I had ever thought *that* was

what skiing was like, I never would have made my first trip."

Everybody's put together differently, of course, especially in the head, but I do recommend that you torture yourself a bit with some kind of flat-land learning before you go skiing the first time. Think of it as a kind of nasty winter tonic like the old springtime sulphur and molasses. You'll feel better for it later.

Friend or Foe

Brace yourself for a major heresy now. *You can learn a lot about skiing from your friends.* I call this a major heresy because all ski books and magazines and instructors constantly rant at you, "Whatever you do, *don't listen to your friends.* If they start trying to give you advice, stick your fingers in your ears and run, do not walk, away from them as fast as you can." The implication is that these friends, most of whom have probably recently gone through exactly what you're going through now and could do considerable to smooth out the bumps for you, are at best simpleminded and at worst malicious sadists. After this kind of thing is drummed into you long enough, you get to the point that when you're skiing you hesitate to ask a friend for the location of the rest room for fear he'll irrevocably louse up your skiing and probably break your leg to boot.

To all of this I say snowballderdash! I agree that you shouldn't rely totally on any one friend to teach you how to ski. In the first place, it's not fair to your friend. He has a considerable time and money investment in the ski trip, too, and he should be allowed to do more on it than follow you around telling you to bend your knees and shift your weight and not to look at your ski tips. You can, however, without actually exploiting your friend, rely on him to save you from some of skiing's greatest troubles and traumas.

Even before you go on the ski trip, you can use your friend to great advantage by letting him show you how to get into your gear. After all, you don't report to your first class nude and barefoot. The instructor expects you to be all suited up and on your skis ready for action. I've long thought there should be a pre-beginning lesson to show you how to put on your boots and attach your bindings and how tight both should be, a kind of Operation Head Start for Skiers, but since there isn't, what else is there for you to do but turn to one of those much-maligned friends? Maybe they don't know everything about skiing, but they do know something, which is considerably more at that point than you know.

It's also a good idea to go on your first ski trip with a friend who has both skied before and skied the particular area to which you're going. There are many confusions indirectly related to skiing that your friend can lead you through with a minimum of time and bafflement. Where are the lockers and how do they operate? Do you get a key at the desk or are they the kind that cost you a quarter each time you close them (in which case you'd better arrive with a pocketful of quarters)? Where do you get the lift tickets? How are they attached? Where does the ski school meet and how far in advance do they expect you to be assembled? Where's the first-aid station (in case you need a Band-Aid and hopefully nothing more)? Where is the ski-repair shop? Where are the restaurants, and, yes, where *are* the rest rooms? (Your nervous state on your first trip will make this the most vital of your queries.) Simple questions, all with simple answers, but you might waste a good part of your first day's ski time trying to find out all this for yourself. I cannot emphasize too much the value of having a friend along on your first trip to show you the ropes—and also the T-bars, the platter pulls, the chair lifts, and the gondolas.

Another thing the friend can do for you is spend about an hour—no more—with you on the morning of your first day before you take your first lesson in the afternoon. Without any danger of teaching you something wrong you'd have to unlearn later, he can show you the following:

1. How to walk on skis.
2. How to get up when you fall down.
3. How to sidestep up a hill—a *very* little hill, one about the size of the sand pile they dump in your driveway when they're doing some minor cement work around your house.
4. How to turn around so you are facing downhill, bracing yourself with your ski poles.
5. How to go down said miniature hill, controlling your "speed" and finally bringing yourself to a breathless stop by pigeon-toeing and heel-thrusting your skis into a snowplow.

All this that you have done with your friend is basically what will happen in your first lesson, and if you've already done it once before, you will have that most important necessity in skiing—confidence. The slope the instructor takes you to will not look like Everest, since you will have already been on one just like it. His instructions will not sound as if they were being given in Serbo-Croatian, because you will have heard something similar before. (You don't hesitate to scream at your friend, "What the hell do you mean, fall line?")

But a word of caution. In fact, a good number of words of caution. Let your friend give you these basics, then thank him nicely and tell him to go away and enjoy himself. You will be better off just playing around by yourself for the rest of the morning getting the feel of things. Maybe if you get your courage up a bit, you can take off from your leaning-on-poles position with your skis together and then slow yourself and stop with a snowplow. That will give you a tremendous feeling of accomplishment, and you will have done it on your own, which is even better. After a certain period of time, friends trying to help get on your nerves. I know. I've had it done to me—and what is worse, I've *done* it. There have been mornings when, after giving my all to help a beginning friend, I've finally been persuaded that I should go take a run. When I returned a while later I always got the triumphant announcement, "How much better I just did it"—the implication being, "without your bugging me." And I'm sure it's true.

The other thing that can happen with friends who hang around too long is even worse. They decide you're beyond all this and decide to take you on to greater glory. Here is a story, the variations on the theme of which I have heard dozens of times. Still, this remains my all-time favorite, because I know personally one of the dramatis personae.

She was a junior at UCLA. She was engaged. She was lovely, and she was not a skier, but since her fiancé was, she was more than willing to learn for both their sakes. In order to give her the ideal introduction to skiing, he decided to make up a party of congenial friends and off they all would go to Alta for a long weekend. Cheerful parting admonition from her parents: "If you break your leg, don't bother to come home."

Scene: Alta. Time: first thing in the morning. He takes care of everything to make sure it's just right. He rents her the perfect boots and the skis with the safest of all possible safety bindings. He leads her over to a small hill and shows her how to make her skis into the V of a snowplow and go down. She manages this with no trouble. "You're great. You're terrific," he says. "I know now why I love you so much. There's no point in fooling around down here where it's crowded. Let's go up on the chair. It's really much easier skiing up there." (The chair in question was not Albion, which serves the beginner hill at Alta; it was the Collins chair, which leads mainly to intermediate and advanced runs, a part of Alta I only ventured into after two years on skis, and even then it was with a certain amount of trepidation.)

After a bit of fumbling toward and onto the loading ramp, he gets her seated in the chair and up, up, and away. At the terminus of the lift she practically skids off the platform to her doom, but is saved by wrapping herself around a convenient post. Still undeterred, he smiles and pats her and says heartily, "That was pretty good for your first time off a chair." (Pretty good? It was miraculous that she got off at all.) Then he is pulling and pushing her along with, "Let's go on up the next chair [Germania]. The run down is even easier from up there." She, full of faith and empty of good sense, dutifully plods and staggers and clumps after him to the next loading platform. Up, up, and away . . . higher and higher.

An old pro now, she exits from the chair with somewhat less difficulty than before. Now they are at the top of the hill, almost the top of the world. He instructs her, "Now we'll go back and forth across the hill. Keep your skis together until it comes time to make a turn and then just do a snowplow the way you did down below and then bring your skis back together again and go in the other direction. There's nothing to it. Don't worry. You have safety bindings. Nothing can happen to you. Just follow me. And, oh, by the way, it might be a good idea if you don't look down the hill. It's not really steep, but it might make you nervous."

He takes off. She places her skis together and starts to follow his tracks cut on the bias across the mountain. She thinks, "Don't look down the mountain," and, of course, her eyes are irresistibly drawn to the forbidden sight. "My God!" She pulls back in horror. Her skis shoot forward increasingly more down the hill than across and faster, *faster*. "If you break your leg, don't come home." "Keep your skis together." "Don't look down!" "Don't come home!" "Keep!" "Don't!" . . . "DON'T!" A waist-high mogul looms in her path. She can't turn. She can't stop. She's going straight for it. The tips of her skis cut into it, imbed themselves and stop. Her body goes on. She flips over the top, her back arching into a *U*. She's certain it's broken. Typical bizarre thought at time of disaster, "Good, I can go home, if it's my *back* that's broken."

Fiancé skids up. Wrings hands and soothes and comforts as best he can. At least he has the good sense not to try to move her. Ski patrol arrives. They bundle her into the litter, covering her entirely with the canvas—head to toe— as is the practice. Again according to practice, they take her down the hill headfirst. There in the dark, upside down, jouncing along in pain and shock, she *knows* they've let go of the litter and any second her skull will be smashed on a tree.

Safe arrival at the bottom. Quick diagnosis: back OK, but knee torn and leg broken just above ankle. Agonizing trip to Los Angeles with leg in temporary cast. Fiancé hovering, grieving, adoring more than ever. She forgives. Adversity brings them closer together. Love is eternal. Happy ending? Not quite.

She had to have an involved knee operation at the UCLA Medical Center to tie things back together and remove bone chips, and she had a *very* long recuperation period in the hospital. And where did this recuperation take place? On the floor where all the other people with knee operations were recuperating. And in a university, who generally has knee operations? Athletes, and more specifically, football players. Since she was the only girl on the floor, she became a kind of team mascot. She was the darling of all and the particular darling of one. Hands across the plaster casts. Broken engagement. New engagement. Marriage.

You've heard the story. Now hear the moral: Our fiancés and friends and relatives love us and think well of us and are overly willing to overestimate our abilities, a willingness most of us share with them. They also enjoy our company, so they want us around to chat with on the lift and pause to admire the view with them on the slopes, and, if they're pretty good skiers, they want us up there where they ski so we can pause to admire *them*. Naturally, they

try to take us along, not just as soon as it is feasible, but way before. Don't succumb to this temptation. Don't make your first day on skis the last day of a beautiful friendship or of a beautiful set of intact bones.

A Lesson on Lessons

Finally, I make what is probably the one statement in this book with which the Professional Ski Instructors of America will agree. You need lessons from good, competent, qualified instructors, and you need lots of them, and you need them forever and ever, amen. There's the agreed-upon theme. Now for my thoroughly disagreed-upon variation.

To Hell with Learn-to-Ski Weeks

Oh, how juicy the learn-to-ski-week packages all sound in their brochures. They are irresistible. They claim to be a fabulous bargain, and that's true. They claim to be a fun-packed holiday, and that's not true. They claim they'll turn you into a perfect parallel skier, and that's a blatant lie.

What a learn-to-ski week is, in actuality, is torturous, grueling work of the sort that if people were required to do it for a living there would be a public outcry and immediate legislation against such inhumane treatment of hapless human beings. Just think of it. Every day for seven days you drag yourself out of bed, every muscle aching (at least, after the first day) and report for a two-hour class lesson in the morning and a two-hour class lesson in the afternoon. And any way you look at it, that's four solid hours of always exhausting and usually discouraging and sometimes hazardous labor. I have seen people limp and stagger in from one of these days so beat they didn't have the strength to take a bath and change their clothes for dinner (after four hours of slope-sweating, believe me, that's tired) and almost unable to chew and swallow. And I confess I have been one of these people. The fatigue you feel in such a situation is not the exhilarating kind you get from a pleasant workout on the slopes, but the leaden, defeated kind you get when you have tried and failed to live up to what your instructor expects of you and what you expect of yourself. You feel at best like weeping and at worst like committing hara-kiri with your ski pole.

As I admitted, though, they *are* a bargain. Your lessons

work out at half or less the usual cost per copy. But the saving in money is flailed out of your vulnerable hide, and therefore, in my opinion, a ski week of lessons would be exorbitant at half the price.

The brochures also emphasize the wonderful feeling of camaraderie that develops between you and your classmates. Again true. You may indeed develop the same kind of lifelong enduring friendships that soldiers who went through the Battle of the Bulge, or Marines who served together on Bataan, developed. Once you've been through utter hell together, it does make for strong bonds.

But there's an unfortunate side effect to this. You hate to look like a coward in front of your buddies, so you do all kinds of brave (read "idiotic") things you wouldn't normally consider attempting. They say you're very unlikely to get injured in a ski class, because the instructor will never ask you to do anything beyond your ability. Probably this is right, but you may ask yourself to do things beyond your ability just to keep your classmates from thinking you chicken. I think what a class basically does is this: on the one hand it holds back the nuts who want to charge down any old hill at any old speed with complete disregard of self and others, and on the other hand it pushes us conservative skiers farther and faster and steeper than we want to go. For them class lessons are safer. For us I have strong reservations.

Personally, I consider it significant that the only time I injured myself (twisted knee that kept me out of action for a week) was when I was on a learn-to-ski week in a class trying to keep up.

You may protest, "But there's no rule that you have to attend every session on a learn-to-ski week, is there? You can skip a lesson or even a whole day, if the fancy strikes

you or you feel they're going too fast." Yes, you can in
theory, but you seldom do it in practice. The first block is
just plain greed: "I've paid for it and I'm jolly well going
to take it." Even if you manage to rationalize yourself out
of that one, you still have a problem getting away. That
comradeship we were just talking about can also produce
severe guilt feelings if you don't show up for a lesson. You
feel as if you were deserting your regiment in the middle
of the war. And top that all off with yet another guilt-
maker: What will the instructor think? I remember once
in the middle of a ski week I reached the "I just can't go
on" point, so I decided to cut class and just enjoy myself.
I found I couldn't. I skulked around the slopes like a crim-
inal, hiding behind trees, afraid I'd run into my class and
have to face up to my defection. I had, I think, an even
worse time than I would have had if I had been in class.

I also remember one night late in the season at Snowmass when I was with a friend who was not even involved
in an actual learn-to-ski week, but she had started taking
class lessons and the instructor at the close of the day
would say, "OK, I'll meet you all here tomorrow morning.
And I expect to see every one of you." The class always
docilely obeyed, so my friend was involved in the same
kind of compulsive situation, just as if it were a learn-to-ski
week. Every evening she moaned and mourned and said
she was exhausted and the class was going too fast for her
and she couldn't stand to take another lesson and swore
she *wouldn't* take one. We even acted out psychodramas
in which she gave her instructor beautiful explanations of
why she couldn't join the class. ("I just got a telegram that
the rabbit died and I'm pregnant, so I'd better not risk
it.") But every morning she would compulsively slog off
and join the group for another day of fun on the slopes,

muttering resentfully to me, "You're not taking lessons. You're just enjoying yourself. It's not fair." An interesting sidelight to this story is that we later found out why the instructor was so pantingly eager to have everyone in class. His contract was up the week before and this one last week was conducted on a you're-paid-according-to-the-size-of-the-class basis. This coercion on his part was actually contrary to the canons of ski-instructor ethics and also contrary to ski-instructor attitudes. Normally, as far as instructors are concerned, the smaller the classes are, the better, so they couldn't care less if you showed up or not.

The worst thing about learn-to-ski weeks, though, is you don't learn all that much. Your mind and body need some time to tamp down what you learn. It's almost like studying a foreign language in that it's better to do it for a relatively short while and then get away from it and come back fresh. In other words, brief, spaced periods of learning advance you faster than one constant session.

As far as I'm concerned, learn-to-ski weeks are the antithesis of skiing just a little bit. Avoid them at all costs—and at all bargains.

Ski Weeks for Weak Skiers

When I come out in violent opposition to learn-to-ski weeks, I don't mean that it's not a dandy idea to go skiing for a week at a time and to attempt to learn how to ski during that period. It's just that I don't think you should go about it in quite the way the resort operators and ski-school directors want you to. I think your week should be a pleasure and not a trauma. I honestly think that if you go about it in my just-a-little-bit way, you'll learn as much, you'll learn it better, and you'll enjoy the process.

There are only a couple of disadvantages to my plan. The first disadvantage is that you have to lie a lot. True, these untruths are only little snow-white lies, and you're only using them for survival, which makes them kind of approved, like stealing bread is OK if you're starving, but still, if you have a George Washington complex, this method is not for you. The reason this lying is necessary is that it's the only way to keep from getting into a class that's not easy enough. And even lying beautifully, you still may have trouble, because a ski instructor told me they always assume adult skiers are one level *higher* than they claim to be, while the kids are two levels lower. That's why in the following outline the lying is almost always accompanied by some dramatic demonstration of ineptitude.

I cannot emphasize too strongly the importance of being in a class that's easy—*too* easy—for you. In fact, your rule should be: *Never take a class lesson in something you don't already know.* Basic new things you should learn not in classes but in private lessons. First you take your private lesson (these are only one hour long) and you learn whatever is for you up the next rung of the ski ladder. Then you learn the little niceties and embellishments the second time around in the classes, where they go more slowly (a class lesson is two hours) and where you can observe others and profit from their errors.

The other disadvantage to my plan is that it costs you a little more money, but that's a small price to pay for peace of mind and wholeness of body. Actually, you may even get more for your money in this scheme, because you are always relaxed and confident, and therefore able to learn what you're being taught. You are relaxed in your private lessons, because you know they will be geared exactly to your level; you won't be pushed to keep up with anybody.

You will be relaxed in your class sessions because you know what's coming. When you're told to do something "new" in class, you will do it with a degree of casual aplomb that will impress your classmates, and—more important—impress you. While others tremble with fear and strain with effort, you in comparison are in control of the situation. It's a good feeling and you ski all the better for it both during and after class.

Here, then, is the schedule:

1st Day

MORNING: Have your friend show you how to fall down, get up, walk on skis, sidestep, and snowplow as described previously. Play around and get to feeling comfortable on skis.

LUNCH: Include a glass of beer or wine to keep the knees loose. (*Note:* Unless you're a minor or a teetotaler or an alcoholic, do not skip this libation. It's an integral part of the learning process.)

AFTERNOON: Take the very basic beginning class lesson. When they place you in a class and ask what you know, say, "I've never been on skis before in my life." To be convincing you might just topple over at this point and lie there helplessly until an instructor picks you up off the snow.

2nd Day

MORNING: Take a private lesson. Unless you're at a major resort where there are some instructors who give *only* private lessons, you'll have to take your lesson early in the morning before the classes start or at lunchtime between classes. Morning is best because then you'll be fresh and you'll have all day to practice what you learn. Morning is best, that is, unless the slopes are icy, in which case it's very hard to stand up, let alone learn anything, so you're better off waiting until the sun slushes things up a little. In this private lesson you should learn linked snowplow turns (that means one after another without stopping in between), and—this is *most* important—how to ride up and get off whatever kind of lift services the easy runs.

LUNCH: Include a glass of beer or wine.

AFTERNOON: Play on the easy runs with your snowplow turns, building confidence both on the slopes and getting on and off the lift.

3rd Day

MORNING: Take another class lesson. Tell them you've only had one (1) class lesson and don't mention the private one. (*Note:* If you're at a small resort with a ski school of only a dozen or so instructors, you may have to let your private-lesson instructor—and you should always keep the same one unless he turns into a monster—in on what you're doing. He'll probably go along with your deception. He's used to all kinds of nuts, and besides, he gets half of what you pay for the private lessons so you're too valuable a commodity for him to reject for minor idiosyncrasies.) If they ask you what you can do, say that you know how to do the snowplow a little, but not very well and, no, you've never been up the lift, but you'd like to try. (Accompany this with a fearful grimace.)

LUNCH: Include a glass of beer or wine.

AFTERNOON: Play around on those slopes with which you're familiar, riding *only* the lifts you've already ridden on. Relax as much as you can and enjoy yourself. If your friends want to play with you *on these slopes,* let them. You might try following them down the hill in order to build up a little speed, but if you consider that they're going too fast for you, forget it. This should be just a nice, easy tamping down of knowledge and fun time. (Another advantage of this scheme over a standard learn-to-ski-week—in those, you *never* have a chance to tamp and have fun.) No sweat. No strain. Keep loose. At this point you're in good control and you're beginning to look as if you know what you're doing, because you *do.* Your friends will undoubtedly try to coax you up onto the highers and steepers, claiming you can easily handle them, which you probably can, but be firm in your refusal. Don't go, because there's a strong chance you could psych yourself out and ruin your skiing for the rest of the week—if not for life.

4th Day

MORNING: Take a private lesson on traversing and the stem turn. Let your instructor take you where he will to do it. It will undoubtedly be where the classes on that level will be given, too. Don't worry if it seems a little steep. He can easily take care of you in this one-to-one situation. (Further note from the Army Ski Accident Report: injury is much less likely to occur in a private lesson than in a class.)

LUNCH: Include a glass of beer or wine.

AFTERNOON: Play at what you learned in the morning in the area in which you learned it, coupled with a few easier runs just for the fun of it.

5th Day

MORNING: Take the stem-turn class. Here you may have to be *very* cagey if you are in an area where they have tryouts for all classes above the snowplow level. When you ski down the hill in front of the instructor who assigns you to classes, be sure you do snowplow turns and only snowplow turns and nothing but snowplow turns. Do *not* traverse. Do *not* do a stem turn. Otherwise you will be flung into the beginning stem-christie class and all is lost. Of course, if this is a place where they ask you where you belong, it's easier. Just say, "I don't know." They will then probably say, "Can you do the snowplow?" Say firmly, "Yes." If they ask if you've ever been up on the lift, say a little bit hesitantly, "Well, yes." If they then say, "Can you do a stem turn?" say, "What's that?"

LUNCH: Include a glass of beer or wine.

AFTERNOON: Play around and impress your friends and begin to feel you are finally really skiing, because you really are. Again, though, do not succumb to the temptation to go whither those friends want you to go.

6th Day

MORNING: Take a private lesson on sideslipping, which is sliding sideways down the hill while in a traverse position, and in beginning stem christie.

LUNCH: Include a glass of beer or wine.

AFTERNOON: Play in familiar areas, but seek out the steeper parts and there practice sideslipping as much as you can stand to. It's just as important as it is boring—and that's *very*. I once had a French instructor who maintained that skiing was *not* turning, but sideslipping. He advised that one should practice it *jusqu'à la nausée*—that is, until you feel like vomiting. I don't quite go *that* far.

7th Day

MORNING: Take the beginning stem-christie class. Again, if there are tryouts do *only* a rather inept stem turn. Do not even hint that you have the dimmest idea of what sideslipping is.

LUNCH: Include two (2) glasses of beer or wine. It's your last day—a celebration—and by now you must have built up a certain amount of tolerance for alcohol in higher altitudes.

AFTERNOON: Relax and do what you like, even if what you like is dozing in the sun on the deck to make sure you have sufficient tan to show off when you get back home. My money, however, is on your being up on the slopes, because you will be totally hooked. Warning: even though this is the last day of the trip, don't make it the last day of the season. Stick to doing only the things you've already done and only in the places where you've already done them. One very good activity for you, incidentally, is to stop a while on the slope and observe the members of the beginning snowplow class flopping around. It will give you a healthy surge of pride at what a long way you've come. Then when it's near the end of the day and there's time for "just one more run," stop and don't take it. You've learned a lot. You've survived. You've had a great time. Quit winners.

Now here's one final rule about lessons. After your first beginning stem-christie class lesson, never take another class lesson as long as you live. Otherwise you cannot possibly avoid being exposed to and infected by Contagious Parallelitis Insidius. It is, however, an excellent idea—in fact, it's highly recommended—that you take at least one private lesson on the many facets of the stem christie at the beginning of each week-long ski trip, or, if you're strictly a weekend skier, at least two private lessons a season.

The program I've outlined here is what you might call the how-to-ski-just-a-little-bit crash program. There is really no need at all to go this fast. You could very logically and sensibly stop with the fifth day's lessons and just play for the last two days, saving the stem-christie learning for the next trip. In fact, if you can control yourself, I recommend doing just that. You could also break up this schedule into weekend bites if you can't get away for a whole week at a time.

HALF THE TRAUMA IS IN THE GETTING THERE

Hemingway in *A Moveable Feast* mourned for the good old days of skiing: "There were no ski lifts at Schruns and no funiculars . . . skiing was not the way it is now, the spiral fracture had not become common then, and no one could afford a broken leg. There were no ski patrols. Anything you ran down from, you had to climb up. That gave you the legs that were fit to run down with."

I go along with him in considering a time without spiral fractures and broken legs as the Golden Age of skiing. I can't however, mourn the loss of uphill climbs. To me ski lifts are a *sine qua non*, but not, alas, a *sine qua non* without tears. My tears flow mainly over the fact that lifts work on a strange kind of inverse skill ratio. The easier the run, the harder the lift that serves it; and the harder the run, the easier the lift.

For example, in most areas, what do you have to ride to

get up the bunny slope? None other than that wrench-your-arms-out-of-the-sockets-and-yank-you-off-your-feet rope tow. And what in the big-time resorts serves the Olympian heights dared only by those kissed by the ski gods? Naturally, a gondola or an aerial tramway, which you can walk onto and off of without either skis or problems.

Only in Taos have I ever heard of a tow designed to require ability commensurate with that required to do the run. As Ernie Blake explained it, "We put in the steepest poma lift in the world. It took off like a rocket and thus reduced the ski-accident rate considerably because skiers who didn't belong on top of the mountain fell off the lift in the first fifty feet. It was insulting, damaging to the ego, but very practical for safety." And that lift, of course, has now been changed.

Because of this inverse skill ratio, I'm of the opinion that in the beginning stages of skiing the lifts are more terrifying than the runs. At least they were for me. I remember in the morning lesson of my second day of skiing I was thrown onto, and subsequently off of, a rope tow, a T-bar and a chair. It was exactly like being asked to solo a DC-8 on your second day of flying lessons. I was reduced to a quivering blob of fear and exhaustion. One thing I *will* say for the experience: it made skiing down the hill seem an easy and pleasant respite in comparison with facing the terrors of the lifts.

Although I've already recommended that you have your first experience on every new lift in the company of a private instructor, I realize this is not always possible. I also realize that even *with* an instructor, the actual getting on and riding and getting off are up to you. Therefore, to prepare you for the ordeal as best I can, I will describe the sadistic peculiarities of each kind of lift. I will also describe as best I can how to master them. I must warn you, though, that riding the various lifts is like giving birth if you're a woman or going into battle if you're a man. It's one of the great life tests and no one can really tell you what it's like. To know your own capabilities or lack thereof, you have to experience it yourself.

Enough Rope

What is a rope tow? It is a rope that tows you if you're lucky and throws you if you're not. Like its predecessors in extermination and torture, the guillotine and the rack, it's really quite a simple device. A motor causes a rope to run on pulleys and a skier holds onto the moving rope and is hauled up the hill. It sounds easy, doesn't it? You just shuffle over and grab hold and skim off, right? Wrong. If you just shuffle over and grab hold, it's as if you tried to punch a judo expert. *Splat.* You're flat on the ground with the wind knocked out of you and no remembrance of how you got there.

What you must do to master the rope is this: Stand next to it, your skis parallel to the direction the rope is going. Slip both poles by their straps onto your outside wrist or, if you're really adept, stick them under your outside armpit. Take your time doing this, fumble around, so that the person in front of you is well along his way. (You don't want to have to worry about someone else's rope-tow problems when you have so many of your own.) Keeping your knees relaxed, put both hands loosely onto the rope (the hand closest to the rope goes over the top). Let the rope just slip through your hands for a minute to get the feel of it and know the speed. Then gradually, slowly, tighten your grip and you're off.

Hold on for dear life and avoid trippable ruts as best you can until you get to what Barnum would call the egress. When you want to get off, remove the hand with your poles on it from the rope, turn your skis slightly away from the rope and toward where you want to go and you will be towed out of the track. Let go of the rope and under your own steam clump and stumble away from the track as fast as you can to get out of the way of the person who is no doubt riding your tail and who doesn't know how to handle a rope tow any better than you do. If you have enough presence of mind to be considerate of others, don't let go with a sudden wild snap. That makes it very hard for the person riding behind you to keep his equilibrium and good nature. Conversely, when someone is getting off just in front of you, be prepared for the rope to flail as if you had a 400-pound marlin on the other end.

When someone riding the rope in front of you loses his balance and falls, don't just hang on and plow him into the snow. Loosen your grip until you stop. (You'll have to still hold onto it with a certain pressure if you're on a hill or you'll slide backwards.) Wait until the dumped one gets out of the way, then tighten your grip and sail off once more. Also when, as inevitably happens, *you* fall, don't just hang onto the rope and plow *yourself* into the snow. Let go and then get out of the way immediately or you will cause something akin to a freeway pile-up.

At most well-maintained resorts there is an instruction sign posted next to the rope tow. This includes one caution that it pays to heed if you want to enjoy a long life. "Do not wear loose clothing" is the way it's often stated. What it means is no long, loose hair or braids or scarves or ties or anything that could get tangled in the pulleys and snatch you bald or strangle you. I heard of a documented story of one woman skiing with a long, flowing scarf around her neck who Isadora Duncaned herself on the rope tow.

When you master the rope tow, then you can take your outside hand off the rope and reach around behind yourself and hold on in that Jackie Gleason "away we go" position, which looks very flashy—at least, it looks as flashy as anything can on something as basically mundane as a rope tow.

T for Two

A T-bar is a device in the shape of an upside-down capital *T*. It is attached to a thin cable which is in turn attached to a thicker overhead cable. Two skiers stand side by side with the cross bar of the T tucked under their derrieres and are pulled up the hill. The flaw in this system is that your troubles are multiplied by two, since there is a pair of human error-perpetrators involved.

The basic steps in T-bar riding are these. You and your partner in crime take the pole straps off your wrists and hold your poles in your outside hands (the sides away from the center bar). The attendant reaches up and pulls down a T as it comes riding along the overhead cable. You and your companion are standing there both alertly looking over your inside shoulder ready to grab hold of the vertical bar when he shoves it behind you. The minute he hands it over, you grab it with your inside hand and with your outside hand you tuck the horizontal bar under yourself and you lean on it. I said lean, not sit. Don't ever sit on a T-bar. I should say, don't ever *try* to sit on a T-bar, because you can't. It seems only the logical and right thing to do, because it's there all tempting and ready and feeling like a nice, narrow little seat to ride up the hill on, but if you do sit on it, it dumps both you and your hapless partner. (See what I mean about double trouble?)

Just after you and your friend start to move on the T-bar, there will be a sudden jolt as the cable runs out its full length. If you are both lightweights it won't be too terrible, but the greater the combined poundage, the greater will be the jerk. Sometimes it is, as a heavy friend of mine calls it, "a real kick in the tail." Be prepared with a good grip on the bar and loose knees.

As you ride up the hill try to keep your skis in the established track. It also helps if you and the other skier keep your inside skis right next to each other, even touching. But whatever you do, don't let your skis cross over his. If you find this happening, put your weight on your outside ski and ride that until you're recombobulated and back on course.

When it's time for leave-taking, it's lovely if there's a route in each direction. That way you and your T-mate can part company with a minimum of anguish. You go your way and he goes his. Almost always, though, the slopes are so arranged that you both must get off in the same direction. The one next to the exit side is the first off and has it easy. He just peels off, but he does have the responsibility of doing so soon enough to allow his partner time to get off before the landing strip runs out. The remaining rider has to first brace himself and the T for the other person's leave-taking. It usually causes a jolt that can throw a body. Then he must disengage himself from the T, and while doing this, twist it so the horizontal bar is parallel to the direction of the overhead cable and then release it gently and gradually upward like raising a window shade. If you snap it up, it's likely to fly around and smack someone, maybe even you. If you're getting off in mid-T (often, especially in the early stages, you won't want to ride all the way to the top), remember to get off and release the T after you pass a tower rather than before so you don't risk tying the T to the tower.

I hate to always look at the dark side but again, when you fall off the T, get out of the way as fast as possible. The T-bar operators should stop it when someone falls, but they frequently slip up. It's not always easy for even a skillful skier to ski around a body on the T-bar path. You can't get back on the T in the middle of the hill. You have to go back down and start all over again.

My own safety preference is to ride the T-bar alone, although that has its balance problems—you have to hold the horizontal bar down very hard with your outside hand. If you must ride two by two, and usually you must, especially on crowded days, in order to have the odds a little more in favor of your reaching the top you should choose a partner at least remotely your size, or else the T will be riding under the rear end of one and behind the small of the other's back. I, 5 feet 2½ inches, 95 pounds, once rode up a steep T with a man 6 feet 4 inches, 220 pounds. The cable ran out its full length as it will when a heavy person is on it, and since it had no more play and I didn't have the weight to hold down my end, it lifted me off my feet and I was left hanging to the bar a good foot off the ground. I don't know what would have become of me if my partner hadn't had the good grace to fall off and restore the situation to at least a halfway normal one.

Although I do generally prefer to ride alone on a T, there is nothing lovelier than riding one with a real pro. He takes care of all your problems for you. That horrible day when I had been so defeated by the lifts in my morning lesson, I was ready to give up skiing. Forever. I meant it. I had a sick, hollow, desperate feeling in my interior that I can only describe as a feeling akin to the homesickness you feel the first time you go away to summer camp. I wanted to quit, but I had paid for my afternoon class lesson (this was back before I hit upon the painless method of learning and was trying to do it strictly with classes) and avarice won out over cowardice. When the bell clanged I lined up. Since I knew I had learned nothing except how to dust the snow off the seat of my pants in the morning lesson, I lined up behind the sign of the level I had already taken—advanced snowplow, I think it was. I had decided if my instructor of the morning (a Women's Marine Corps drill-instructor type) approached the group, I would discreetly split. But no, there came to us a slender young man, soft-spoken and with a slight accent. I thought he was Austrian, but he said later he was Dutch. He introduced himself as Art and said, "So, now we will go on the T-bar." My soul shriveled within me. "But don't worry," he went on cheerily, "I will ride up with each of you for the first time." This at least was something, but I was still not what you would call at ease.

When my turn came, I stood next to Art as loose and relaxed as a bronze casting. My hand rigor-mortically gripped the T. We lurched off. "But you are so tense," said Art in his soothing Droste chocolate voice. "You must relax. Here, hold my hand. There is nothing to be afraid of." He peeled my hand off the T-bar and held it gently but firmly as we skimmed up the hill. He maneuvered me off at the top so gracefully and easily that I didn't even know it was happening. All I remember is his saying, "See, you can do it. It is not so hard." And then he was skating off down the hill for the next passenger, as I stood there with waves of adoration washing over me. May your first T-bar ride be just like this. More I cannot wish you.

J-Bar

J-bars are just like T-bars except they are shaped like a right-side-up *J* and you ride them alone, which makes them lovely. The only thing wrong with J-bars is that you'll almost never find one. Resorts usually choose to put a T in over a J every time because with the same investment in poles and cables, they can double their lift capacity with a T.

Served Up on a Platter

A platter pull, sometimes also called a poma, looks as if you took a T-bar, bent it a little, cut the crosspiece off, and attached instead a flat, slightly oval disc approximately six to eight inches in diameter. You stand at the ready just the way you would waiting for a T- or J-bar, the attendant hands you the platter by its vertical bar, you stick it between your legs with the platter underneath your seat, the cable stretches out, jerks slightly, and off you go. In order to keep the jolt from throwing you, you're better off holding onto the bar with your full weight until that jerk takes place, and *then* settle back against the platter for the rest of the trip. At the end of the ride, disengage yourself from the platter and hold onto the bar with your inside hand until it's time to let go and leave. Needless to say, you hold your poles—straps off the wrists—in the hand that's not holding the platter pull pole.

There are no problems unique to the platter pull except

in some of the French resorts where they make right-angle turns and sometimes even go downhill for brief stretches. No daydreaming allowed on these.

Old Rocking Chair's Got You

I recently heard of a psychiatrist in New York who was starting hypnotherapy sessions for people who have an irrational fear of flying. He said that the irrational fears connected with flying are things like acrophobia (fear of heights) and claustrophobia (fear of being closed up in a small space). He believes that these irrational fears can be eliminated with hypnosis. On the other hand, I gathered that the fear that the plane may crash and you may be killed dead is quite rational and hence must be worked out some other way than by hypnosis, like maybe with martinis.

As far as chair lifts are concerned, if your fear is the irrational fear of height, all I can recommend is using either hypnosis or True Grit. The latter *is* possible and it *does* work and you *do* eventually get over your fear. Three different people I have lured into skiing had such extreme acrophobia that they all virtually swooned on the second step of a stepladder. But through sheer determination—they really wanted to ski—and sheer sloth—they really didn't want to climb the hill to do it—they overcame their terror.

If, however, you have the perfectly rational fears, such as the one that the chair may knock you over when you're trying to get on or that you may break a leg trying to get off, then I may be able to be of some help.

When getting onto the chair, make sure you and your partner have enough time to get into position before the

chair gets there so you won't be all off balance and confused when it does. The heavier one should ride the side of the chair closest to the lift towers. (If you ride alone, also ride closest to the lift towers.) Side by side, knees bent slightly, ski poles (straps off wrists) held in outside hand, look over your inside shoulder to see the chair coming. When it's there, hold your inside hand down to block the chair slightly so it doesn't whack you in the back of the legs—very bruise-making. Slide on and take off. Remember to keep your ski tips up, since there are often mounds of snow in front of the loading platform that can trip you up and flip you out.

I'm sure you wouldn't be idiotic enough to deliberately rock the chair, as you're riding, but if you're going up with someone who finds it great sport, tell him off before he shakes you off. Hold onto your poles carefully while you're riding. If you dropped one on a skier below, it would be murder.

Some chairs have a footrest that is raised by lowering an overhead bar or swung into position by a handle. These can be tricky, so unless either you or your lift companion knows how to work it, just let your feet dangle. If you *do* use the foot rest, be sure you disentangle yourself from it in plenty of time to get off. There are usually signs warning you, like doomsday prophets, that the end is near. Again, be sure you keep your tips up as you approach the loading platform.

As you leave the chair, there is often, in fact, usually, a ramp you have to ski down. This always looks about three times steeper to you than it actually is. Your every instinct tells you to pull back, and just as always in skiing, your every instinct is wrong. Pulling back will only cause your skis to shoot out from under you. What you must do is, as you leave the chair, scoot up to the edge of the seat and when you get to the place where you're to get off (there's usually a sign for that, too) lean forward and push yourself off with your inside hand against the seat of the chair. Still leaning forward, ski down the ramp, slowing yourself, if necessary, with the good old reliable snowplow. Keep moving until you are out of the way of others who will be getting off behind you. Should you perchance fall, creep and drag and slide yourself out of the way as fast as you can. Chair-lift operators, like T-bar operators, are supposed to stop the mechanism when there's a body in the path, but they, too, are only about 50 percent reliable.

One of the most important things to remember about getting off the chair lift is to be decisive. If you hesitate, the perfect moment is past and the leave-taking will be harder or even impossible. In some chairs, if you freeze and don't get off you're in real trouble. You can't just ride up around the machinery and down the hill again. They have to stop the lift and remove you from it. I once saw this happen to a girl. She was marooned in the chair six feet up. Two strong men had to come over and, one holding each leg, lower her to the ground. This was much more hazardous and humiliating than getting off sloppily or even with a fall.

After you feel comfortable on the chair, you can relax and smoke, if you're addicted to that unnatural habit, or eat snacks or blow your nose or do anything you feel like doing. But beware as you fumble in your parka pocket. A friend of mine once let a twenty-dollar bill flutter to the snow below. As it turned out, this wasn't as disastrous as it sounds because she was able to ski down and get it before someone else did. In fact, it did wonders for her skiing speed, because although normally she skis in a slow and careful manner, her descent this time resembled some of the more thrilling scenes of *Downhill Racer*.

Easy Riders

If you can walk, you can ride a gondola (a small four-to-six-person cabin that rides on cables) or a cable car (a huge cabin holding forty or fifty persons, sometimes called an aerial tramway or a téléférique). In the former you stick your skis into the receptacles on the outside and take your poles inside where you (*ahhhhhhhhh*) sit down and rest and enjoy the view, assuming that you've already worked out your little acrophobia problems on the chair lift. In the latter, you walk in carrying your skis in an upright, non-fellow-skier-smiting position. Unless you're first in and can get onto the bench that runs around the edge, you'll probably have to stand, but at least try to get next to a pole to hold onto in case of sudden lurches, which there always are, especially at the takeoff.

Good Liftsmanship

Rule one is you don't cut lift lines and you don't invite friends to sneak in and join you unless you're a bona fide single waiting to ride a lift that takes two, such as a T-bar or a chair.

The cry of "Single" that you hear echoing around the lift area is the signal that someone is looking for a partner. On crowded days, on any lift that takes two you have to go two by two ark style. To be polite you usually have to accept a perfect stranger who wants to ride with you, no matter how imperfect he may appear to be. Once I saw a fellow in his early twenties bashing hell-for-ski-wax down the hill toward the end of the lift line, all legs and arms and ski poles and speed and chaos and noise. As soon as he crashed to a halt he split the air with the cry of "Single." No response. Everyone in the line looked frostily in the opposite direction. Finally, in exasperation he shouted again, "Single! Single! Aw, come on, folks, don't worry, I ride the chair a lot better than I ski."

At the end of a ride on a chair or a T, if you and your partner have survived the experience, it's customary to bid each other farewell with "Have a good run." And very likely you both will. After all, the hardest part of the run is over.

3

Three to Make Ready

When you begin to consider thinking about your first ski trip, there are three kinds of preparation you have to make. Two of these, getting your equipment and clothing in good shape, are relatively pleasant activities. The third, getting yourself in shape is, to put it mildly, ugh. First the ugh.

SHAPE UP BEFORE YOU SHIP OUT

The way to become a really terrific and marvelous skier is to start getting in shape for winter sometime around Memorial Day by jogging five miles before breakfast every morning, methodically going through the *Royal Canadian Air Force Exercise Manual*, giving up smoking and drinking, getting eight hours sleep a night, and taking up yoga. Isn't it fortunate, then, that you have no intention of becoming a really terrific and marvelous skier, but only intend to ski just a little bit, and therefore don't have to go through all that grisly torture euphemistically called preseason conditioning. Not that it wouldn't be marvelous for you if you did. You just don't *have* to. I figure I may as well tell you you don't have to, because if you are the kindred spirit you must be to have read this far, you wouldn't do it if the sanctity of your bones depended on it.

But, really, you should do something to get yourself at least a little bit ready for a sport that ranks equal in energy output to football. You should do something, that is, besides just thinking about exercise and groaning at the thought. Here then in descending order of effectiveness are some possibilities.

Calisthenics

Good news. Should you by some miracle of determination clamp your jaws together and enter into a serious preseason exercise regime, there are three of the classic little horribles you can skip, because they aren't even good for you. They are: the deep-knee bend (it can actually damage and weaken your knee joint); the toe touch (it can injure the spine); and the swan (it can damage the lumbar region).

Some of the exercises that are, I'm sorry to say, good for you and good for your skiing are push-ups (from the knees only for women), sit-ups (done with knees flexed), and three-quarter knee bends. There's another exercise I recommend for women who wear high heels a lot, one I even do myself in strong moments. This is the Achilles tendon stretcher. The Achilles tendon is that thing running down the back of your leg, and high-heel wearing scrunches it up. In skiing it has to stretch, and the pain is intense if it

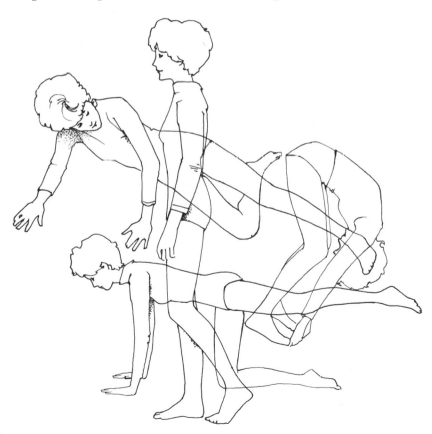

hasn't been loosened up in advance. Using a stair step or a strong ledge like a raised hearth, balance yourself on the balls of your feet and let your heels drop down below the ledge. Then pull them up to the level of your toes and let them drop down again, then back up on the toes, down on the heels, etc. Don't try to do this exercise without holding onto something or you may lose your balance and have a living-room ski accident.

By the way, if you are really out of condition and over thirty, don't do any of this conditioning without checking with your doctor. If you want to be a casualty, save it for the slopes, where there's more drama involved.

Jogging

This is separate but equal in value to calisthenics. In fact, some say it's the best preparation there is for skiing, since it builds up the heart and lungs and circulatory system and increases their capacity to handle that spectre of the slopes, stress.

A while back there was such a jogging craze that a friend of mine trying to jog at night in a small park near her home encountered a human traffic jam every evening and once even suffered a head-on collision. A doctor predicted early on that because it's basically such a boring activity, the mania would soon die down, and so it has, but if you have a high boredom threshold and can stand the tedium, it will do wonders for your endurance both on and off the slopes.

There is a way of cheating at jogging. This might be called jogging for the diffident, for those who can't bring themselves to make the sweatshirt scene on the public streets and sidewalks. You simply stay indoors in the privacy of your own home and run in place. For it to do the most good you have to keep up a speed of 75–100 steps per minute, counting one step each time the left foot hits the floor, and you have to work up gradually to the breathtaking (and on the slopes breath-making) pace of 1,500 steps in fifteen minutes. But then, if you do your quarter hour of running in place regularly every day, you can consider this a total program.

Fun and Games

The trick here is to make your workout play. In other words, make what you do to get in shape for skiing something you'd enjoy if, horrible thought, skiing had never been invented. This is, I realize, similar to telling you that you should take Latin in order to learn English grammar, but as anyone who has ever taken Latin will tell you, it works and so does this. My favorite activity that fits into this category is bicycle riding. It's not terribly strenuous, especially if you have a light bicycle with gears. It strengthens your legs and improves your heart, lungs, and circulation capacity. It also gets you out in the fresh air—if such exists in your community—and it lets you see a lot of sights you normally miss when you flash by in the car. But if bicycling doesn't appeal to you, there's always tennis, bowling, horseback riding, golf, swimming, and so on through the whole lexicon of sports. Just make sure it's something *you* enjoy and something you'll go out of your way to fit into your daily life.

Walking

Even if you're a hard-core lethargist to whom fun and games are not fun and games, maybe you'd be willing to go along with a little walking to get in shape. It's free, it takes no equipment, and you don't have to stand in line to do it. True, you may have to fight off friendly drivers who will stop and offer you a lift, because no one can believe you're doing it because you *want* to. In our automotive society, where it's beginning to seem as if we've been grafted onto our cars, even neighbors who would probably just look the other way if they saw you being mugged or raped are immediately moved to compassion at the sight of your pedestrianization. Walking may also make you fall under suspicion. In certain communities—Beverly Hills is a notable example—nocturnal perambulators are regarded as potential criminals (why else would they be walking?) and are often challenged by the police and sometimes picked up. Yes, it takes courage and determination to be a walker these days.

If you decide to walk, walk whenever possible and do it at a good clip. Don't just meander. You'll find it one of the best all-around exercises there is. For even though it may not be exactly true that if you can walk, you can ski, at least it is true that if you *will* walk, you will ski with a great deal more ease.

Stair Climbing and Rope Jumping

You won't walk, huh? Well, really, it's not so much that you *won't* walk as that you're too busy to fit it in. All right, then, are there any stairs in your home or in the place where you work? Could you manage to keep yourself out of the elevator a few minutes every day? Climbing stairs is the greatest conditioner and calorie burner of them all, greater even than chopping wood. A regular amount of stair climbing can do magnificent things for your heart and lungs—and your legs. If you are truly dedicated to conditioning yourself, you can double the effectiveness of your stair climbing by hopping up with both feet together, turning them slightly to the left on one step and slightly to the right on the next. This approximates wedeling on skis (an advanced form of very short parallel turns straight down the fall line)—not that you're intending to wedel on skis, but it's a terrrific exercise if you don't mind getting caught at it and being regarded as an eccentric by apartment neighbors or office colleagues.

No stairs anywhere? All right, jumping rope is almost as good. And it's a good way to use up your old clothesline. Start with about twenty-five or fifty jumps, depending on your condition, and slowly, gradually—say, about five more a day—work up to two hundred.

Move a Little

You're still fighting it? OK, then just go ahead and do what you're already doing, which is to say practically nothing, but try to desedentaryize yourself a little. Get out of the static and into the motion habit.

I know a man (whose name, in the interest of marital harmony, I won't mention) who before every ski season swears he's going to lose twenty pounds and really get in shape. He even indulges in sporadic jogging and weight-lifting sessions, but otherwise he never moves a single muscle if he can possibly avoid it. He drives in the car everywhere he goes. At work he remains sitting in his chair and will scoot it across the floor on its rollers with his heels rather than get up and walk five feet to the files. At night he drops into his easy chair and requests that his drink be brought to him. He does manage to walk to the dinner table, but once there he sits as if strapped in for air turbulence. Should he desire something missing from the table —salt, fork, or whatever—he asks for it rather than get up and fetch it himself. After dinner he re-sinks into the easy chair, where he remains immobilized for the entire evening.

A lot of men are like this. Perforce their jobs are sedentary, and not so perforce they make their whole way of life the same. We women are a bit luckier. The housewife's job is nonsedentary, involving as it does lots of bending, stooping, stretching, squatting and trotting. The marathon existence of housewives builds up their endurance without their even realizing it. For this reason, in the first ski lessons the seemingly frail wife often does better than her seemingly brawny husband. As any marriage counselor can tell you, this is disastrous and should be avoided, even if it takes a bit of nagging.

Mechanical Monsters

Some of you who look over these relatively mild conditioning possibilities may say, "I'd like to do them all, but I know myself. I won't. I lack will power." And then you may start eying the ads in the papers and magazines for exercise mechanisms, such as exercycles and rowing machines, mechanical jogging tracks and I don't know what all, but I do know how much all—very expensive. You think you're buying willpower, but you're not. If you don't have the willpower to do any of the other exercises, you won't have it to work out on these contraptions either. No matter what the ads say, they are even more tedious than other methods of exercise. They will only turn out to be a source of embarrassment to you as they stand there in the middle of the room and rebuke you for your sloth until you give up and move them out of sight. It is ridiculous to spend vast quantities of money on this junk. You should save your vast quantities of money for the junk more directly connected with skiing. Believe me, you'll need it.

Skiing Makes the Heart Grow Stronger

Remember, one of the very first features of skiing is that while you're doing it, if you do it on a regular basis, you don't need to do any other exercises to stay in excellent condition. If a sport can deliver you from the excruciating boredom of exercise for four or five months a year, that alone is enough to recommend it, isn't it?

IN HIGH GEAR

This may disappoint you, but I'm not going to recommend running right out and buying all your ski equipment at once. After all, there is always the microscopic chance that you might not like skiing. I will even confess that one (and *only* one) of my converts flamed out on me after the first day. His reason for giving up was that although he has the torso and legs of a man of 6 feet 3 inches, he has the arms of a man of 5 feet 5 inches and consequently cannot reach down to fasten his boots. It's pretty hard to argue against something like that, so I didn't. Luckily the only thing he had bought was a beautiful blue ski sweater, and this was not a waste, because he can wear it to the more casual bars on his circuit.

Another fellow I heard about wasn't that lucky. Since he was fairly athletic, he was so sure he'd cut a flashy swath that he went right out and bought the best of everything —skis, poles, boots, bindings. The day after his first day on skis, which was a dismal failure due to a bad case of athlete's ego, someone got a remarkable bargain in some slightly used ski equipment.

My advice, therefore, is to rent everything in the way of equipment for your first trip. After that, if skiing takes— and you'll know immediately if it has or has not—then you should buy everything, because in the long run it will be cheaper than renting and it's much better to have the same equipment every time you ski so you'll be used to its idiosyncrasies.

The drawback is that at this point you won't know what you really want in the way of equipment, and you probably won't know until you've had a season or maybe even two under your stretch pants. I could tell you what I like, but that wouldn't mean that you'd agree. In fact, you most probably wouldn't. Skiers, even us just-a-little-bit types, are independent people with strong likes and dislikes who will argue for hours over different brands of ski equipment as passionately as wine experts fight it out over vintages. For this reason I'll just give you a few tips to help you get stuff that won't unduly hamper your learning or jeopardize your safety, and yet it won't be a financial disaster for you when you inevitably chuck it out sometime during your second year when you become the world's greatest living expert on ski equipment.

Boots

As everyone will tell you, boots are the keystone of your equipment and should be your biggest investment. This does not mean, however, that if you march out and plunk down $150 or so for highly touted (in advertisements) something-or-others, you can't go wrong. On the contrary. You could be in mortal agony every moment you're in them, because, now hear this, the really important thing about a pair of boots is not how much they cost, but *how well they fit.*

Last year I spent a month going around the ski shops with a friend of mine who needed new boots. Very early on she found a pair of Nordica Comets which were pure pedal paradise for her, but she resisted buying them because they weren't expensive enough. She had had it in mind to "step up" and spend about one hundred dollars for boots, yet these poor waifs at $52.50 were the only ones she felt happy in. And she was in a position to recognize happiness, having had a season of misery with a pair that ground her ankle bones and froze her feet. She had come to fully understand that legendary comment, "Taking off your boots at the end of the day is better than sex." Finally, after trying on every pair in her size in Los Angeles and its environs, she wisely decided that money was no object, bought the Nordicas, and has been constantly delighted with them.

Although it's true that you're better off with a $35 pair of boots that fit than with a $135 pair that doesn't, how do you know at the beginning stages whether a boot fits or not? Ay, there's the rub, and the rub often makes blisters or bone spurs. I can tell you how they say boots are supposed to fit. It sounds something like this.

1. A boot should feel tight, but it should not hurt at any one point. The buckles should snap shut in the middle notches, not the first (too wide) or the fourth (too narrow).

2. You should be able to wiggle your toes, but there

should not be too much space at the end of the boot. Your toes may even touch the front of your boots when they are unbuckled, but buckling will push them back enough so that they don't.

3. The heel should fit snugly below the ankle bone but not pinch.

4. The boot should give firm enough lateral support so that the ankle cannot bend inside it. This is very important, because your knee movements need to be communicated directly to your skis.

I trust all of this boot-fitting jargon is about as clear to you as it was to me before my first season—which is to say, not very. But read it over two or three times and try to muddle through the boot-buying experience the best you can. It helps if you can find a ski shop with a knowledgeable fitter who doesn't just try to con you into the most expensive pair in the house—and lots of luck to you there. It also helps if you have the patience to try on dozens or scores or hundreds of boots if necessary to find a pair that feels good (but not too good; you're after boots, not carpet slippers). Don't be embarrassed, either, if you try and don't buy. Ski shops are used to this and they'll just think you're a discriminating purchaser.

One point to remember when you're trying on boots is to whack the heel of the boot down hard on the floor before you buckle it. This forces your heel back into the proper position in the boot. Not only do you have to do this to see if the boot really fits, but it makes you look as if you've maybe tried on boots before and know what you're doing, which *may* discourage any boot-fitter fraud they have in mind.

No matter how careful you are, it's still very difficult to get a perfect fit in the first pair of boots you buy. For this reason I recommend that in this initial purchase you stick to leather boots rather than investing in the newer plastics, because:

1. They're cheaper.

2. They're easier to have pressure points punched out of when you suddenly discover they feel miserable after scuffing the new off on your first trip. Yes, yes, I *know* the new plastic boots have all kinds of miracle squish inside that conforms to every foot bump or little sacks of soft that can be shifted for individual ecstasy requirements, but take my word for it and hold off on these until buying your second pair.

3. They're more yielding. Until you're a fairly experienced skier, you simply don't need boots as stiff as the plastics. Maybe you'll never need them if you keep up your membership in the just-a-little-bit club.

Plastic *soles*, though, are very good. They resist curling up at the toes like harem slippers, even when they're sopping wet and you forget to put them in a boot tree.

Be sure, also, to buy buckle boots and not the kind that lace. Lace boots are almost obsolete now and very time-consuming. You probably don't need to have double boots (laces inside, buckles outside), either, unless you have chronically poor circulation.

Finally, if you should find yourself with a new pair of leather boots that turn out to be uncomfortable, I offer you, for what you think it's worth, the following suggestion from Frank Day, author of *If You Can Walk, You Can Ski*. (Warning: Don't read this if your boots only hurt when you laugh.)

Skiing in new boots can be painful. Here's what you can do about it: Before taking a bath put on the two pairs of socks you would ordinarily wear while skiing. Put on your boots, lace them up and get into the tub. Stay there for half an hour. Get out of the tub, dry yourself, put on a bathrobe and walk around the house in the wet boots for two hours. You may need someone to follow you around with a mop, but it will be worth it. The boots will mold themselves exactly to the shape of your feet. Take them off and put them on the boot clamps. Stuff them with newspaper; this will absorb the moisture. Put in fresh paper as needed. It will take several days for the boots to dry thoroughly, but if the above directions are carefully followed your boots will fit comfortably.

Skis

Most beginners spend too much on skis. It's an area of equipment buying in which you can really save, especially when you're a novice. Considering what you'll be doing the first season, you don't need "instant obedience" or something that "tracks like a bullet" or "is precisely engineered for super-skiing" or "the hottest thing put together."

Even the names of skis like Javelin and King Tiger and Atomic and Perfection Super and Wedelking and Slalom Racer put a body off—at least, they put this body off. I've often thought it a shame that some ski manufacturer doesn't recognize the needs of us just-a-little-bit skiers with a whole line of special skis just for us. I can almost see the ads. . . .

IF WINTER COMES, CAN DERRIERES BE FAR BEHIND?

In keeping with its tradition of providing something for everyone, the Derrière Ski Company proudly announces its new fall line of skis. No ifs, ands or buts, Derrière skis can get to the seat of your skiing problems and bring them to a safe end. Just look at what's coming out of the back door of our factory this year.

The Scaramouche

Extensive study of the peculiar needs of the retreating World War II Alpine troops, combined with a rigorous testing program at Mt. Tremblant, have resulted in this triumph of ski design, the Scaramouche—the ski for professional cowards. With its colorful chicken decal on the front and its wide yellow streak running back to its distinctive "turn tail," this ski is the ideal visual complement for the truly intimidated.

But there is more to the Scaramouche than meets the eye. Its gelatin center core makes it possible for your every knee knock and tooth chatter to evoke an immediate emphatic shuddering response beneath your feet.

Exclusively for use on the Scaramouche the scientists of Derrière Laboratories have formulated a new "Slo-Base," which assures the inveterate "piste-creeper" that he will never pick up speed, no matter what the snow conditions—from fresh powder to solid ice. Not only that, but with a modicum of careful waxing the Scaramouche can easily be made to actually adhere firmly to the snow and **not move at all** on slopes up to 30°.

The only question now is, are you mouse enough for the Scaramouche?

The Blubber King

Pleasingly plump or a downright fat slob? Then this is the ski for you— Derrière's new ЖF (King Farouk) special posthumous autographed model of its ever-popular Blubber King. The distinctive exaggerated curve of the shovel makes it possible for you to keep your eyes fixed on your tips as you ski, no matter how great may be your girth.

This year Derrière has added yet another exclusive to the Blubber King for your skiing pleasure: under its peelable plastic coat there is a sandwich construction of corned beef on rye with mustard laminate for those whose appetites tend to get out of control on the slopes far from the lodge's snack bar.

And remember, with each pair of)F Blubber Kings you get our unconditional money-back guarantee that your every fall while wearing them will produce only royal purple bruises.

Believe us, once you try Blubber Kings you will never abdicate!

The Smart Ash

The only wood ski in the Derrière line, this is the ski with a mind of its own, scientifically engineered for the skier who doesn't know what he's doing on the slopes.

Unresponsive, uncontrollable and totally unforgiving, the Smart Ash will drag the hesitant, blundering skier through turns and down slopes completely against his will, always chattering loudly with its distinctive refrain, "Lemme tellya whatchur doing wrong."

Skiing the Smart Ash will bring a new surge of adrenalin to your system and cause new color to flame in your cheeks.

Remember, when it comes to skis, **everybody** loves a Smart Ash.

The Sitzmark

If you are one of the legion of skiers who spend over half their time lying in the snow recovering from a fall, at last here is a ski just for you—the Sitzmark, the only ski designed exclusively for comfort and manageability while the skier is in a prone position. The Sitzmark has a truly original cube shape, which enables the skis to remain flat on the ground whether the skier is lying on his right side, his left side, flat on his back, flat on his face, or is, in unusual cases, upright.

Also available on the Sitzmark are the "Golden Hind" optional luxury accessories, such as a built-in transistor radio, brandy flask, and inflatable pillow, all for the additional pleasure of the skier who is a master at reclining on the slopes.

Test-rest this unusual ski on your dealer's floor today. Who knows? Maybe this will be your season to fill your Sitzmarks.

The Lounge Lizard

This is the ultimate. Years of patient resort research have produced what we consider to be the total ski for the compleat nonskiing skier. The Lounge Lizard's unique single-unit construction—two skis joined together at the base with a secret resin-and-epoxy formula—makes it absolutely impossible to ever separate them from each other.

Lounge Lizards are carefully weight-engineered for jaunty over-the-shoulder carrying. They stack easily in any kind of ski rack or they can, because of their unusual built-in "thrust power," be inserted tail first in snow banks and remain standing when more conventional skis are slipping apart and clattering to the ground in an untidy heap.

Home storage is no problem for camber-free Lounge Lizards. They can be kept anywhere: in an unheated garage, under the bed—even leaning them against the furnace will in no way diminish their performance.

For superior lodge-deck status it is recommended that you buy Lounge Lizards at least 15 centimeters longer than normal and mount them with long thong bindings.

Don't weight—or unweight—any longer. Find your place in the sun this winter with Lounge Lizards.

DERRIERE MFG. CO. LTD., U.S.A., FOGGY BOTTOM, WASHINGTON, D.C.
Derrick Derrière, Pres.
John & Frankie O'Rear, Technical Consultants

But until Derrière Skis opens its back doors to skiing pleasure there are several solutions available to you for acquiring your first pair. For instance, you can watch the want ads of your local throw-away newspapers and the cards on those little racks in the supermarket. You may be lucky enough to find a disgruntled refugee from the slopes like the fellow I mentioned a little while ago. Skis, like cars, plummet in price after their first mile of use.

If you live in an area where there are a lot of skiers, you can watch for the preseason ski swaps. Some of these are held by ski clubs, some by sporting-goods stores, and some in conjunction with ski shows. In general, the way they work is that those who have something to sell pay a nominal fee (ten or twenty-five cents) for a two-part ticket with a number on it. On half the ticket the seller writes the price he's asking and attaches it to what he's selling. He keeps the other half. If and when the item is sold, the buyer gives the money to those in charge of the business end of the swap and they put it in an envelope and file it by ticket number. The seller then claims the money by presenting the other half of the ticket.

I was skeptical about the merits of these ski swaps until I went to my first one and sold for twenty dollars a pair of boots I had bought two years previously at an end-of-the-season clearance sale for thirty-five. Now, not surprisingly, I consider swaps the greatest boon for skiers since the invention of the safety binding. Another thing ski swaps should do for you, incidentally, is inspire you to take good care of your equipment, which, of course, you should do anyway. At swaps a pristine-looking piece of equipment or clothing is always sought after, if not actually fought over.

Although I did sell my boots at a swap, I really don't recommend buying boots at one unless you know at least a little bit about what you're doing—that is to say, until you've been skiing at least a season. Your first pair of skis, though, could easily come from a swap. If they have a good base and don't look so slummy that they'd be an embarrassment, and they're the right size for you, I see no reason not to snap up a bargain. At some ski swaps the ski shops put out last year's model of brand-new skis at a good discount. Since often the only difference between two seasons is a name (as when Hart shifted from "Holiday" to "Jubilee") or a different decal, you can often get a real buy.

Often, too, ski shops with rental departments will sell off their rental equipment at the end of the season. That's how I got my first pair of skis. Old Hart Standards they were, and I got two good years out of them before I felt the pressing need for five centimeters more length and a base I didn't have to wax all the time. Incidentally, I gave these skis to a new convert and they are still going strong —or should I say *weak?*—since she, like me, is a dedicated just-a-little-bit skier.

There's another good source for buying your first skis. Some well-known ski manufacturers—Fischer is a notable example—still make wood skis. These cost only thirty or thirty-five dollars, and since the firms are good and experienced ones, the basic design of the skis is excellent. In fact, if I were starting skiing right now, I think these are exactly what I'd buy. Also, if you buy with care you'll probably be able to find a pair with a running base of P-Tex or the like that is just as good as the most expensive models—and maybe even with interlocking edges, which a lot of skiers set great store by. These skis are brand-new, and so, of course, they look lovely, and they will probably serve you admirably for a season or two until you can pick out your big-time models, drawing from the vast wisdom of your experience.

Incidentally you needn't make apologies for skiing on humble woods. Most skis are wood-cored anyway. The fiberglass or metal of the other models is just the main load-bearing material which makes skis stronger and, most experts say, perform better. But that kind of sensitive performance can come later, when you'll be able to notice it.

And what about that great current battle between fiberglass and metal? At the moment I'm part of the great metal army. Since I whack them around a lot both in my sloppy skiing and in my flight bag, I like the durability of metal skis. I've heard that although fiberglass skis tend to lose their camber and chip more readily, skiing on them is easier than on metal. If this easy skiing be true—and I may rent a pair to find out—I could easily become a defector to their legion, since to me easy skiing is everything.

Length? Everyone will tell you something different on this. I think Irene Kampen sums it up nicely in her *Last Year at Sugarbush*.

The correct length of the ski is of vital importance. Test for proper length by holding one ski up vertically beside you, its tail resting on the floor. Now stretch one arm straight up in the air. The ski should reach to your wrist, or to a little below your wrist, or to the middle of your palm, or to your outstretched fingertips, or to the crest of your iliac, depending on whether you are listening to Rick Shambron, Fred Iselin, Ornulf Poulson, the editor of *Ski* magazine, or Cliff Taylor, the shortski man."

I won't hesitate to throw in my opinion, either, and at least my opinion will have the advantage of being beautifully definite. When you ski just a little bit, your skis should reach two or three inches beyond your elbow when you hold your arm above your head. If you are on the heavy side, make it four inches.

Would You Want Your Sister to Ski on a Pair of Short Skis?

As for those really short skis—or shortskis, as they call them—I think they look dumb and I wouldn't ski on them. Oh, for a gimmick at one of those resorts where they teach you by increasing your ski length daily; but buying them I think would be, to coin a phrase, short-sighted.

HELPFUL HINT: Buy a couple of those little rubber straps with metal clips on the end. You use these to hold your skis together, base to base, which makes it easier to carry or stack them. While you're skiing, the straps can be stowed in your parka pocket.

Bindings

Contrary to the sound of the name, bindings are not what you use to wrap up dislocated knees and gushing wounds, as I thought when I first heard the term used in conjunction with skiing. On the contrary, if they work properly, they will do a lot toward preventing the above mishaps. Bindings are the mechanisms that under normal conditions hold your boots onto the skis and under abnormal conditions, such as a fall, release your boots from the skis so you won't get hurt. Most modern safety bindings have two parts: the heel holder and the toe holder. And when I refer to bindings, I do mean safety bindings; ancient bear traps and modern nonreleasing long thongs do not even exist as far as I'm concerned. Also, I do mean step-in bindings rather than cable bindings. Forget the cables. They're outmoded, except for rental-shop use, where their ability to change size easily is an advantage. For you the non-ability to change size easily is an advantage. People are much less likely to ask to borrow your skis if they know it means major binding surgery.

The basic rule on bindings is: Buy the best, no matter what they cost. Fortunately this is one case where the best is none too expensive—around fifty dollars. I know that may sound like a lot, but when you compare it with what you can pay for the best in boots and skis and when you compare it with the cost of a broken bone or a knee operation, it's nothing. Besides, you can keep your bindings forever, shifting them from old skis to new skis whenever you wish.

When I say buy the best, I don't mean just the highest-priced. I mean the safest. And what binding might that be? Frankly, I don't know. I'm no engineer, and on top of that I'm a woman, which means, according to the sexual stereotype, that I am totally a-mechanical. Any remark I make about bindings is likely, in fact *certain,* to make "experts" from coast to coast writhe and rant and vomit. But as President Johnson said when he took office, "I will do my best. That is all I *can* do." And you know how well things worked out for him.

Mainly because I've been so interested in the sanctity of my own bones, I have read virtually everything written on the subject of bindings and I have talked to the binding men in almost every ski shop in Los Angeles (that means at least ten of them). I have grilled every ski instructor I've come across and I've listened to any crackpot who wanted to sound off. Here then is a distillation of what I've learned and experienced personally.

In general, the question of what is the safest binding has, as the psychiatrists like to say about their questions, no right or wrong answer. It's just what you feel. Most of the ski instructors I've talked with recommend Markers or Look Nevadas. At the moment of this writing I'm skiing with the Marker Simplex toe in combination with the Marker Rotamat heel. Of course, this choice is partially because I'm extremely susceptible to ski-instructor advice and also, a little, because I like them for the reason that, although they're sometimes awkward to get into on the flat, they're easier to put back on when you're lying down in the snow after a fall.

I feel obliged to warn you that one of my converts broke her leg while wearing Marker bindings. She exonerated her Markers, though, claiming it was because her boots were too loose in the heel to transmit the fall impulse well enough to make the bindings release. Incidentally, her daughter, who uses Look Nevadas, sustained a bad knee injury the same season. Her mother claimed this was because she had them adjusted too tightly. I wouldn't, however, consider these two mishaps an indictment of either binding. Maybe it's more of an indictment of the family as being ski-accident prone.

Looks and Markers and most of the other big names on the market are what they call "lateral toe and vertical heel releasers." In other words, they'll let you out in the three most common directions of falls—forward and to each side. They don't work for backward falls, but the fact that your knees bend the way they do when you fall backwards takes care of most problems there. My friend who broke her leg on the Markers said she was looking over her shoulder to see if the coast was clear to make a turn when ɪᴛ happened, so possibly that particular fall was in one of the nonreleasing directions.

There *are* bindings that give you a so-called all-directional release. Millers and Cubcos and Gertsches fall into this category. *Consumer Reports* has been quite enthusiastic about the safety of all-directional-release bindings, but don't mention *Consumer Reports* to ski-shop people or you'll be subjected to a sneery "What do *they* know about skiing?" One ski-shop man cautioned me that no all-directional-release binding is good for skiers above the strictly recreational level, thinking, I guess, that that would put me off. Little did he know.

I have been told that even these all-directionals have their little problems. Millers and Cubcos, for example, require the addition of metal plates to the boots. These can get scratched and battered when you walk around in your boots and hence have to be replaced or the releasing mechanism of the binding is impaired. Millers are also so complicated to install that few ski shops will tackle the job, and those who will charge a ten-dollar installation fee. As the kind of person who always takes out the maximum flight insurance, what I like most about Miller's Ambassador model is that the manufacturer *guarantees* you won't break a leg while wearing them and they pay up to five hundred dollars if you do. They also sell a model called the Miller Supremes (seventy-five dollars) which pays up to a thousand dollars for a broken leg—that is, if the binding is factory mounted. For these, their advertisement states, "Sold for twelve years with more than 3000 pairs in use . . . . and *without so much as a pulled muscle reported!" That* impresses me.

I have friends who are tremendously loyal to and have never broken anything on their Cubcos. Cubcos are relatively inexpensive (standard, $19.95; black Teflon-coated deluxe, $28.95) and can be installed and adjusted in most ski shops. Irene Kampen made a lot of fun of Cubcos in her book as being not very status-y, but then she made a lot of fun of everything.

This season I had just about decided to turn in my Markers and switch to what I had decided was the safest of all the all-directional bindings—the Gertsch. These are impossible to describe—you have to see them—

but their distinctive feature is that your boot fits on a boot-sole-sized metal plate, and when release takes place, the entire plate goes, taking your boot along with it. Since the release does not depend on the shape or condition of your boot, I would *think* this would mean the ultimate in reliability.

But just when I was steeling myself for the fifty-six-dollar outlay of cash for the Gertsches (fifty dollars for the bindings and six for installation) I read about the new Spademan. This is an entirely different binding concept, so different, in fact, that they don't even call it a binding but a release system. It is unique in that it has no toe piece. It was designed by a doctor who was concerned that many injuries result from the boot's being momentarily blocked by the toe piece in a forward fall, before release can take place. No toe piece, no blocking, and fewer broken limbs.

I was able to inspect the Spademan (fifty dollars) in a local ski shop that had been selected to preview it. I was so impressed with its obvious merits—compactness, ease of entry, ease of adjustment—and by its manufacturer's claims of giving all-direction-release safety for all levels of skiers that I feared whatever I might buy this season would become obsolete in another year, if Spademans prove in actual use to be as ideal as they seem in appearance and theory. Rumor has it that Lange, too, is on the verge of marketing a toe-pieceless binding. And who knows what other new binding ideas will suddenly burst on the early seventies scene? I think I'll just hold onto my Markers a while longer and wait and see. Like Scarlett O'Hara, I'll think about it tomorrow.

But whatever I decide, I intend to find out all I possibly can about available bindings before I make my decision. After all, my bones are at stake. You should have exactly the same attitude about your bones. That's why I definitely don't and won't recommend to you any specific brand of bindings. I refuse to take the responsibility. You should read a lot of articles on bindings, you should talk to skiers and ski instructors and ski-shop men who appear to have good sense, you should think a lot, and, in the final analysis, you should pray a lot.

But even the most careful selection and the most ardent of prayers won't help you if your bindings are not properly adjusted. Just as in boots the fit is all, in bindings the adjustment is all. If they're too tight, they won't release during a fall; if they're too loose, they'll release while you're executing a perfect maneuver and you'll flip out. You should have your bindings installed and adjusted in a ski shop that has the proper equipment and know-how, but you should also read the instructions that come with them so you can adjust them yourself if you have to—and often you do. Just toting your skis up to the ski area on the rack of your car can get your bindings totally out of whack.

Once when I went to Europe my first station, as they call resorts over there, was Lech in Austria. The jouncing of the flight must have done something funny to my bindings, because when I got out on the slope they released every time I took a step. I hied myself to the basement ski shop of the Hotel Tannbergerhof and tried to explain my problem in my nonexistent German to the young attendant. He listened seriously, took a screwdriver in hand, and ever so carefully tightened my heel bindings as tight as they would go, while I watched in silent horror. Luckily I knew more about adjusting them than *that*, so after I got outdoors again I took a schilling and unscrewed them to a sane point. When you do adjust your bindings yourself, do it a little on the loose side. Although ski-accident reports indicate that as many accidents result from bindings releasing too soon as from those releasing too late, you're very unlikely to wham them loose on a turn in your normal course of skiing when you ski just a little bit.

Friction Makes the Binding Grow Weaker

Another fairly recent development to help us skiers in our eternal quest for reliable binding release is the antifriction device. They've discovered that one of the main reasons why many bindings do not release or are slow in releasing is friction between the boot sole and the ski. Slowness in releasing can, you know, be quite as bad as not releasing at all, since the bone can snap while it's waiting for the sluggish release. Several manufacturers have come out with devices to be placed on the ski under the ball of the foot to eliminate this friction. Two of the best are the Rosemount Lotork and the Cubco Skidder, but new ones are coming out all the time.

These don't work for everyone, or maybe it's just that they're not necessary for everyone or, more likely, not available in a proper size for everyone. I myself was so inspired by all the articles on the importance of antifriction devices that I raced right out and tried to get them put on my skis. But the shop refused. Since I wear a size four boot (don't laugh; so does Nancy Greene), the Lotork, which I was attempting to buy because it doesn't require lubrication, would have been beneath practically my whole foot instead of just the ball. The fellow in the shop said to forget it and he also said that I needn't worry, because in my Markers the toe of my boot actually only contacted the ski in a very small area, so there was hardly any friction likely to be set up.

I accepted his advice, but I will keep the top of my skis where my boot rides waxed and clean and slick, and I probably *will* worry until they come up with a junior-size antifriction device that I can use or until Gordon Lipe, the binding-release expert, personally checks me out and says I don't need one.

Speaking of Gordon Lipe, there is available for the careful skier (isn't everyone?) a portable Lipe Skier's Release Check, which measures how much force it takes to knock you out of the toe piece. Naturally, there's a table to tell you what the force should be, based on your weight and skill. At around fifteen dollars one of these would seem to be a worthwhile investment, especially for a skier who travels a lot and is likely to get his skis out of adjustment on car roofs and in ski flight bags.

Safety Straps

Safety straps can logically be mentioned in conjunction with bindings, since they are invariably used in conjunction with bindings. These straps are also sometimes called "runaway" straps because that's what they prevent—runaway skis. If you fall and your binding releases and there is no safety strap keeping your ski with you, off it races down the hill. A runaway ski is a lethal weapon, but even if the idea of skewering your fellow man is not enough to make you invest the three dollars or so that safety straps cost, then maybe the thought that without them you could lose or break your valuable ski will inspire you to make the expenditure. And if that doesn't do it, remember that most ski areas now won't even let you onto a lift without safety straps. Wise move.

There are single straps that you clip onto the binding and onto the boot, but I don't care for these. They have a loosely hanging loop that very well might catch on something, and also in a fall they don't prevent the "windmilling" of the released ski.

Far, far better are the Arlberg straps. Besides having an attractive name, they (you use two on each ski) crisscross over your boot and look at least slightly long-thongy, which is good for your image.

Two safety tips for safety straps: 1. Don't buckle them too tightly; that is, don't tug at them with all your strength to try to force them over just one more notch. If you do you may impede the releasing properties of your bindings. 2. Be sure to buckle your Arlbergs on the outside rather than on the inside of your feet. Who knows—someday you may accidentally find yourself making a traverse with your ankles locked together and the buckles could catch on each other and spoil everything.

Poles

The poles you buy can be beautifully cheap unless you're a real heavyweight who would bend them into parentheses as you heave yourself out of the snow if they weren't made of tempered steel, or unless for some reason you require the kind that double as elongated brandy flasks. The only thing you really have to worry about in poles is what length to buy. But that's not so easy to decide. Each season pole-length fashion changes. The current style is to pick poles that when stuck in the snow will keep your arms from the elbow to the hand exactly horizontal to the snow's surface. Of course, since you won't be buying your poles out on the slopes, the way to test them in the shop is to turn them upside down and, placing the grips on the floor, grasp them under the baskets. Then if your forearms remain horizontal to the floor, you've got the right size—at least for a season or so.

For my part I prefer poles a little on the short side to force myself to bend my knees more, but that's a personal aberration not necessarily to be accepted as a normal way of ski life.

SNOWSUITABLES

As a Southern Californian I had to buy new every last thread needed for my winter vacations. If you dwell in a colder part of the country, you'll be either more or less lucky, depending on your personal attitude toward shopping and money spending. At any rate, if you don't have them as a regular part of your wardrobe, you'll need, along with wool slacks, a heavy sweater, and warm gloves:

1. A warm coat. Any kind will do, but for the ultimate in chic get a sheepskin or shearling coat—woolly inside, suedeish leather outside. Morland, an English firm, is one of the names in this field, but there are others. If your local stores don't stock, you can write for catalogs from Abercrombie & Fitch, Antartex, Deerskin Trading Post, and Norm Thompson. You'll find their addresses in the appendix along with names and addresses of several other mail-order companies. You can use these sources for anything in the ski- and cold-weather-attire line that you can't find in your own community.

2. Snow boots. These are called after-ski boots by us phonies and *après-ski* boots by those even phonier than we. When you try them on in the store, remember to try them on with ski socks, which are what you'll generally be wearing with them. Be sure the boots you buy have soles that are of some substance that the wet won't soak through, and look for some extra-thick kind of corrugation on them to keep you from falling on the ice. Otherwise, just as driving to the airport is the most dangerous part of flying, walking up the icy steps to the lodge can be the

most dangerous part of skiing. Also, be sure your boots come up high enough to allow you the luxury or the stupidity of stepping into a deep snowdrift or slush pool.

These clothes aren't to ski in; that takes a lot more specialized attire. These are for before and after ski, and they're not just for comfort, but for actual survival. I've seen the anguish on the faces of my fellow Los Angelinos on their first mountain trips, as slush fills their loafers or soaks their tennis shoes, and as icy wind easily breaks through their lightweight "windbreakers." I once observed two blue-tinged boys in jeans and light sweaters whose permanent mountain position—I think they were frozen in place—was arms crossed over their chests with fingers held firmly in armpits for warmth. Warm clothing is as vital off the slopes as on, maybe more vital, since while you ski you become your own central-heating system.

Incidentally, if you do go to a ski resort and find yourself inadequately attired, either off or on the slopes, don't hesitate to buy anything you need there. I've checked it out carefully and although I know it's hard to believe, ski clothing and equipment cost no more at even the jet-settiest resorts than they do in ski shops down on the flatland. This is not because resort prices are so low, but rather because ski-shop prices are so high.

But now to the basics of your wardrobe for skiing itself. What must you have in the way of clothing if you intend to ski? I can give you the answer in one word: everything. You need this everything even if you're only going to be an occasional skier. If you become more of a regular at it or if you happen to be extremely clothes-conscious, you'll need, or at least want, several of everything. Here, then, from foot to head is the basic Everything for Everyskier.

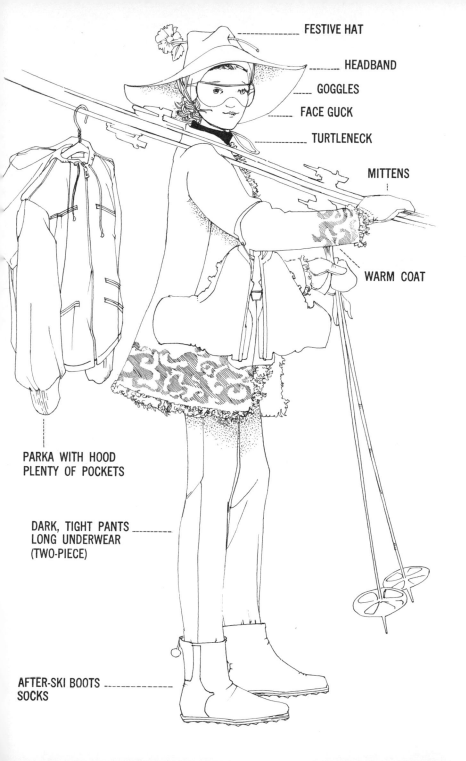

FESTIVE HAT

HEADBAND

GOGGLES

FACE GUCK

TURTLENECK

MITTENS

WARM COAT

PARKA WITH HOOD
PLENTY OF POCKETS

DARK, TIGHT PANTS
LONG UNDERWEAR
(TWO-PIECE)

AFTER-SKI BOOTS
SOCKS

Socks

Socks have to do with that all-important factor, comfort. They pad the foot to keep the stiff boot from making sore spots and they provide warmth. Cold feet in the figurative sense are normal on the slopes; in the literal sense they are an unnecessary hazard.

The first decision is whether to wear a single pair or two pairs. I will mention straight off that a fellow who *looked* knowledgeable in a ski shop once told me, "Wearing two pairs of socks is a good way to break a leg." I didn't give that much credence, because I figure that at least half the skiers, often including me, wear two pairs—a pair of lightweight socks next to the foot and a pair of heavies over these. The next decision is what should the socks be made of, and here is your choice:

Wool (used singly and as outers)—still the basic warmth-maker. Skiers prefer Norwegian ragg socks, which vary from 85 percent to 100 percent wool and cost only two to three dollars a pair.

Thermal (used singly or rarely as outers)—these are insulated socks of nylon and wool. The price increases as the wool content rises:

70% wool, 30% nylon—$1.95
75% wool, 25% nylon—$3.00
80% wool, 20% nylon—$3.50–$4.00

Wicking (used as inners and outers)—made of magic fibers like polypropylene or olefin. These are called "wicking," because they do not absorb moisture, but rather pull it away from the foot like a candlewick drawing melted tallow to itself. The inner socks cost two dollars a pair and the outers cost from three dollars to six dollars, depending on the wool content. The six-dollar variety has 65 percent wool and 35 percent olefin.

Cotton (used as inners)—absorbent and lightweight, the poor man's silk. Very cheap and easily obtained.

Silk (used as inners)—absorbent and lightweight, the rich man's cotton. Obtainable only in ski and sports shops at two fifty to three dollars a pair.

And while on the subject of socks, I will now pass out to you a piece of counsel that I consider second in importance only to forgetting trying to learn to ski parallel. It is this: Put on your socks *before* you put on your ski pants. Not only is it more comfortable this way, but it is vital that you do it for more subtle reasons, as you will see from this bit of . . .

SOCKS EDUCATION

There's this guy who's six four
With a cleft in his chin,
Dark curly hair
And a lopsided grin,
And yet with the girls, he hasn't a chance,
For he wears his socks outside his ski pants

He can schuss like Killy
And wedel like Stein,
In each race he's always
First over the line,
But out on the slopes, no one gives him a glance,
Since he wears his socks outside his ski pants.

His prep school was Choate,
He's a Harvard man now,
And his family arrived
In the Mayflower's prow,
But he's dropped by the Blue Book and looked at askance,
For he wears his socks outside his ski pants.

Two inches of wool
Turn a prince to a lout,
You're in if they're in,
And you're out if they're out,
So if you seek status and long for romance,
You must sock it to them *inside* your ski pants.

Tom Swift and His Electric Socks

Yes, they do exist, but I mention them mainly to warn you off. At least, *I* would never wear them for skiing, she said coldly. I can't imagine what would happen to the wires squashed inside your damp ski boots. On second thought, yes, I can imagine. But more important, the batteries, which are carried on the back of your upper calves like tiny knapsacks, would wreck the line of your stretch pants. Still, since their vendors *call* them ski socks (could they possibly mean after-ski?) and claim great things for them, who am I to thwart the American free-enterprise system? You'll find a couple of mail-order suppliers listed in the appendix. But if you use them, don't have your heirs contact me for wake money.

Underwear

Oh, yes, you will, too, need it, no matter how hotly races your blood or how undignified you consider long underwear to be. You will definitely need a full complement of classic long johns. In warmer climates and for spring skiing you may not need the tops—and mercifully, long johns do come in two pieces these days—but I find it's always more comfortable to have the bottoms on under your ski pants.

There are several different kinds of underwear that work well, so you can be guided by your personal aesthetic taste, if such a term can be used in conjunction with something as basically unaesthetic as long underwear. Any ski shop can put you next to—and vice versa—Duofold or Ski Skin thermal underwear. Both are made of two layers of material. Duofold combines a soft cotton inner for absorption with a mixture of wool, cotton, and nylon outer for warmth. Ski Skin inners are 50 percent cotton and 50 percent Quintess polyester (whatever that is, it is supposed to give strength and resiliency) and the outers are 30 percent wool and, here we go again, 70 percent Quintess. The advantage of these two brands is that they are available in bright colors and prints so you don't look like Charlie Chaplin in *The Gold Rush* when you wear them, and also they are machine washable. The prices range from five dollars to seven dollars, depending upon whether they are uppers or lowers; white, solid color, or print; and which brand you buy.

Warmer still would be something with more wool like Duofold's Viyella (55 percent wool) or all wool. If you are a world traveler or happen to have a Chinese cousin, the all-wool kind can be purchased at rare bargain prices in the back alleys of Hong Kong. The Hong Kongers, though, unfortunately don't make you look like Suzy Wong. In fact, the husband of a friend of mine who wears Hong Kong wools enjoys at social gatherings mentioning how funny, *really funny* Kaye looks in her underwear and chuckling at the reminiscence. This is, as his wife says, the kind of thing that erodes a marriage. But if you feel your marriage is erosion-proof, Hong Kong wool is very warm.

Another highly touted warmer-upper and -lower is wearing underneath your regular underwear a layer of that rather unusual all-cotton Norse net underwear which looks as if it is made of loosely woven string shopping bags. Its holes are supposed to trap the warm air next to the skin. I can't vouch for it personally, though. I've never tried it, mainly because it doesn't come in women's sizes—yet another example of sexual prejudice in our modern age. But

I can easily sourgrape the Norse nets away with the knowledge that they show a pattern through your ski pants, and that would *never* do.

If you want the Cadillac of long underwear, you can buy—or possibly lease—Duofold cashmere (15 percent cashmere, 75 percent wool, 10 percent nylon) at $12.50 to $13 *each* for uppers and lowers. If the Cadillac isn't quite good enough for you, there's always the Rolls-Royce, silk. The one source I've seen for this is the Orvis Company (see appendix). The price is $18 for the bottoms and $16.50 for a short-sleeved T-shirt top.

As a final luxury-underwear idea I offer this tip from a skiing rancher's wife. (They spend three solid months out of every year at Alta, where often the cold is piercing, man, piercing.) Her suggestion is somewhat akin to Zsa Zsa Gabor's helpful hint on how to use up your leftover caviar, but, anyway, "Save your old cashmere sweaters to use as underwear uppers."

Pants

It is said that Willy Bogner's invention of stretch pants did more to popularize modern skiing than anything else, including the safety bindings, and I believe it. They are indeed a boon, albeit an expensive one. At least, they should be fairly expensive if they're going to last you more than a season and not ball up or bag out. As Irene Kampen says, "The buyer of cheap stretch pants can be easily identified on any ski slope by his bagging knees, drooping seat, flapping ankles, and sagging waistband. There is one brand of stretch pants that retails for twelve dollars and has been officially recognized by our State Department as Japan's answer to the atomic bomb."

When selecting your ski pants, get them about one size tighter than you think they should be, unless, of course, you have some physical reason not to, such as diabetes, in which case you shouldn't be too tightly bound around the waist. They say ski pants should be tight enough so that if you put a dime inside in the hip area, you can see through the fabric whether it's heads or tails. The rancher's wife had a tip on stretch-pants buying, too. If you can't find a pair that fits exactly, then get a pair that's too small and let them out rather than a pair that's too large and has to be taken in. She says the too-large ones can never be made to fit properly. I agree with her. I had a pair of too-large ones once that I had in and out of the tailor's three times before I finally gave up and gave them away. They always bagged somewhere or other.

These particular pants had an additional problem. They were bone-colored. Bone-colored ski pants are gorgeous in ads and almost irresistible in ski shops but always a total mess on the slopes. In ten minutes you look as if you've been mining coal in them. Skiing is a clean sport, but no sport is *that* clean. Stick to the darker shades, unless you happen to own a dry-cleaning establishment. I also dis-recommend ski pants with racing stripes down the side for the likes of us. Not only are they harder to match up with sweaters and parkas, but on skiers of our ability they're grotesque, rather like Grandma Moses driving a Maserati.

Over-the-boot pants are very "in" now, which makes me feel like opening a vein, because I have four relatively new pairs of the into-the-boot *fuseau* variety. (Let that be a lesson to you not to overbuy in any style.) The over-the-boot kind are not as practical as the others, since in deep snow they can get packed up, but they are more comfortable and they look great, giving you that much-sought-after long, lean line. And, anyway, who ever let practicality interfere with good looks? Remember, though, when you're shopping for them, take along your boots, lest you buy yourself a pair of over-the-boot pants that won't.

Novelty pants like knickers and lederhosen (available from Outdoor World and the Swiss Cheese Shop) are fun for a change and they do give a lot of freedom of movement. Another couple of popular and good-looking styles these days are those coverallesque jump suits and those one-piece jumperlike pants-top combinations. I've never tried these, because, to tell the truth, it would look to me as if the restroom operations, already formidable, would become impossible.

Another pant item you may want in your collection are those which are variously called "warm-up pants," "storm pants," "wind pants," and in Utah "powder pants." These go on over your regular pants in extra cold or snowy weather. They are made of a very light water- and wind-repellent synthetic and come in solid colors, navy especially, as well as the new wild psychedelic and hippie flower prints. Some models—I recommend these—have zippers running down the sides of the legs so you can put them on or take them off without removing your skis. Many of these come with a carrying pouch into which you can fold them up and carry them along on your parka belt to be prepared for a sudden change in weather. I've seen these pants as low as twelve dollars (for the single layers, in Morzine, France) and as high as twenty-two dollars (for the warmer double layers, in the U. S.). It appears that a little shopping around would be advisable.

Thrift note: a young man told me that he always skis in blue jeans with warm-up pants on the outside and claims

he's never cold and has great freedom of motion. And, as he points out, who knows but what he has a pair of eighty-five-dollar Bogners on underneath? (Edification note: Do you know what blue jeans are called in skiing circles? Oklahoma Bogners.)

One final bit of down-to-earth ski-pants counseling. Should you perchance break your leg, try to keep your wits about you in the first-aid station and see if you can get them to cut open your pants leg carefully along the seam so it can later be restitched. A broken leg is expensive enough as it is without adding the cost of your stretch pants into the bill.

Turtlenecks

I suppose you *could* wear something besides a turtleneck —a wool shirt or blouse perhaps—but I can't understand why anyone would want to. I'll admit that I'm prejudiced. I adore turtlenecks. I wear them constantly all winter, whether I'm skiing or not. With them I'm almost like a cowboy with boots. You have to practically cut them off me with a case knife when summer comes. My idea of pure luxurious wealth would be to own every color and pattern of turtleneck made by every manufacturer. And wealth it would have to be. Each year the price of turtlenecks shinnys up another fifty cents or dollar. I attribute this to their increasing popularity among non-skiers who have discovered their comfort and versatility. These days they can be worn for every occasion from painting the garage to a formal reception. I also suspect that some of these earth-creeper turtleneck wearers are trying to pass for skiers, but I may be accusing them unjustly.

It's true, though, that a turtleneck, more than any other item of attire, except possibly your boots, makes you look like a skier, and feel like one, too. Get several in different colors and wear them while you ski and for after-ski and while you are at home to remind you of the slopes. They come in cotton and in synthetics like nylon polyester and Banlon. The cotton ones have the advantages of costing less and absorbing more perspiration and hence of being a little more comfortable to ski in. They have the disadvantages of fading—especially in darker colors—and shrinking into funny shapes, often a kind of hiking up in the back. The synthetics are vice versa: they cost more but hold their color and shape, and they can get a little slimy when you exert yourself. What I usually do is ski in cotton turtlenecks (even if they're out of shape, it doesn't show under all the other stuff you're wearing) and use the synthetics for after-ski when appearance counts for more. When I go on a long trip I take only synthetics, because they're more compact for packing and are also easily and quickly washed and drip-dried.

Sweaters

There's not much to say about these. Everybody knows what a sweater is and everybody has his own taste in them. My own preference is for a crew neck because it looks so nice to see your turtleneck (there goes my obsession again) poking out the top. I consider turtleneck sweaters too bulky and scratchy, since skiing involves a lot of neck-screwing around. My personal favorite sweater is one I ordered from Shannon Airport (see appendix). It's one of those heavy off-white natural wool Aran Island or fisherman's knits in which the wool is unscoured; hence a lot of the oil is left in for warmth. The semi-noncolor goes with everything, and if you're the sentimental type you'll enjoy the card that comes with it saying that your sweater was hand knit by Bridget O' Something-or-other in County McWhatchamacallit. The only thing wrong with these sweaters is that there are a lot of cheap imitations on the market these days, but once you've seen the real thing, the difference is obvious.

Another good sweater source is Norway. I have a friend of Norwegian ancestry who visited the old sod—or as they would put it, *den gamle land*—and checked out a couple of sources, Husfliden and Kløver Huset. She got her lovely Norwegian sweaters for only around sixteen dollars because she was there, but if you order directly from this country, they are still only a little more than twenty dollars, which is a noticeable saving, since in stores over here they run forty to fifty and even sixty dollars, if they are available at all, which the ones from Husfliden aren't.

A third supply house—that of Norm Thompson—is the home of unique Cowichan knits, "the world's most treasured sweater that is an original work of art." These are made by a small Indian tribe in British Columbia of undyed, unbleached, homespun wool in natural shades of white with black, gray, and brown designs. The company claims that such personages as Queen Elizabeth, Prince Philip and Bing Crosby are all proud possessors of Cowichans.

Of course, your best sweater bet is if you are a knitter or have a knitting friend, wife, mother, aunt or grandmother, because then you can have a true original made to your own color design and size specifications.

Gloves and Mittens

During my early skiing days I had the same attitude toward gloves and mittens that I had toward Bordeaux and Burgundy wines during my early wine-drinking days. I had heard that the sophisticated and refined palates

prefer Bordeaux, and so, automatically assuming my own sophistication and refinement, for years I would never let Burgundy touch my lips until once, traveling in Burgundy, I had no choice but to drink it unless I wanted to be stoned to death on the spot. To my amazement, I found I *adored* Burgundy—liked it much better than Bordeaux, in fact, and I have been devoted to its consumption ever since.

What happened with gloves and mittens was that I heard that skiers who want sensitivity of control with their poling *always* wear gloves. Don't ask me why, when my own pole action has all the sensitivity of control of a five-year-old stabbing peas with a fork, I felt I should wear gloves, but ego plays funny tricks, and I did. As a result, during my first season I almost froze my fingertips off. When I finally switched to mittens it was like a draught of warming Burgundy and I became an instant addict. Stick to mittens. Forget about sensitive control. Sometimes even mittens, where fingers get together to pool their warmth, can be not warm enough and you'll need additional inner mittens of wool or silk.

For skiing in knuckle-frosting climes the best solution of all is down mittens. Although they cost as if they were filled with spun platinum and, puffed up as they are, they make you look as if you're skiing in boxing gloves, they are the only total warmth I've come across. If your ski shop can't supply, Eddie Bauer can at about fifteen dollars. The kind made by Weiss cost five to nine dollars more, depending on your friendly ski shop's markup, but they have the advantage of being leather all around instead of just in the palms. Also, if it does anything for you, the tag on the Weiss mittens says Weiss is the exclusive supplier to the U.S. Ski Team (although the team probably uses gloves, since sensitivity of control *is* important to them).

The other advantage gloves are supposed to have over mittens is that you can do vital things like adjusting your bindings and blowing your nose with them on, while with mittens you have to take them off and expose your fingers to the chill. I disagree. In my glove-wearing days I found I had to remove them to do anything involving any more dexterity than making a snowball.

I won't entirely condemn gloves, though. I'll admit that I wear a light pair for spring skiing to avoid sweaty palms caused by heat (fear-caused sweaty palms nothing can be done for).

All gloves or mittens, of course, must be leather or some reasonable facsimile thereof or, in the case of down mittens, have leather palms at least, so they don't get soggy in the wet and won't wear out immediately on rope tows.

Parkas

It takes at least four years to learn to stop saying "ski jacket" and start saying "parka." The reason I give this particular time cutoff is that I've been skiing for three years now and, try as I will, I still use the non-skiing term occasionally.

What makes a parka a parka is the hood. Somewhere on or in every parka there is a hood for you to put on when the weather turns around. Sometimes it hangs loose down inside the back. Sometimes it's folded up and put into a pocket—usually an inner one. Sometimes it's even rolled up and hidden in the collar. I still remember a new recruit of mine who came stumbling into the lodge with her five-dollar hairdo matted with new-fallen snow, cursing her lack of hat, when all the while her hood was lurking there inside her parka collar.

What kind of parka to get? Two kinds. Leaving the aesthetics of the selection up to you, you need both a heavy parka and a light shell, if you're going to be prepared for the different kinds of weather you're likely to encounter in a season—and sometimes in a day or even in an hour. Your heavy parka should most definitely be a down-filled one. These are light and warm and you'll eventually feel you absolutely must have one, so you might as well get it in the first place. It's an idea to buy your parka a little on the long side so that it insulates everything from where the neck bone's connected to the collar bone and the thigh bone's connected to the hip bone. Since down has that famous "breathing quality," there are those who wear their down parkas in even relatively warm weather. Still, when it warms up, I prefer to ski in something lighter, like an unlined shell with a sweater underneath. In really hot just-before-the-thaw spring skiing weather a wind shirt with a turtleneck underneath is most comfortable, unless it's reached the point that it's actually bathing-suit weather.

By the way, parkas can have an added use for the skier. They are very good for predicting weather changes. If you wear your lightweight parka, the moment you get onto the lift and head up the hill, the weather turns bitter, freezing cold. While if you wear your heavy parka, the sun immediately breaks through the clouds and the temperature shoots up to 85°.

Pack-a-Parka Pocket

Luckily, parkas have commodious pockets, because there's a whole gang of things you'll want to carry along.

First off, there's tissues. Skiing makes the nose run even when you don't have a cold and, of course, you may be crying a lot. You should also have some kind of lip lubricant, since you'll be doing a good deal of nervous lip-licking. Suntan lotion or cream would also be of use to recoat yourself with occasionally, or to be a good samaritan with if you see a fellow skier starting to blister up before your eyes.

Although I usually don't chew gum, I carry it with me when I ski to help counteract my perpetual dry mouth (there are no drinking fountains on ski slopes). A friend of mine who has diabetes always carries small boxes of raisins and foil-wrapped dates and dried figs for quick insulin counteracters. I think this is also a good idea for nondiabetics. Skiing with low blood sugar is hazardous for anybody.

For sociable types a pencil stub with a blunt point and a small notebook are useful for jotting down names and addresses and phone numbers.

A small hunk of wax of the kind you use with fresh snow is also of great value. Even if you have one of those bases that "don't need waxing," they definitely do need it in the fresh stuff, which can really fasten itself to a ski bottom and cement you to the slopes.

Naturally, you must also carry money. Skiing is the original bring-money sport. You'll want coins as well as bills, since most ski bindings can be adjusted with a coin.

Hats

Besides keeping you warm (did you know that approximately one-third of the body heat escapes from the top of the head?), a hat expresses your unique personality. Who am I to say whether you are a cowboy or Tyrolean or deerstalker or Cossack type? Almost all the mail-order catalogs in the appendix have a wide selection of weird head coverings for you to choose from. And each resort seems to have its own distinctive headgear. For example, spring in Snowmass brings out big high-crowned, floppy-brimmed, flower-print sun-keeper-offers for the women.

One of the most versatile of toppers is the stocking cap that unfolds into a combination hat and face-mask-like covering for the mouth and neck and ears. A brushed-wool version of this, called a Balaclava helmet, is available from L. L. Bean.

But whatever hats you affect, it's also wise to have a few headbands in your collection. These keep your ears nice and warm under hats in really cold weather and in not-so-cold they can be worn alone, if you like to let your hair blow free. They are also good to stick in your parka pocket for emergencies when you think it's going to be warm, but it isn't (the heavy/light parka weather rule holds again).

Sunglasses and Goggles

Definitely yes. Vital. You can really fry your eyeballs on the slopes on a sunny day. Snow blindness is not just a myth. And do get something of a good enough quality to be comfortable, unless you enjoy headaches, and something unbreakable, unless you're a fan of eye operations.

On a snowy or cloudy day, yellow lenses are essential to lighten up the scene. On an overcast day you sometimes get a weird flat light in which you can't see the bumps, and unless you have trees to orient yourself with, you don't know up from down. One fellow (leg in cast) I talked with in the lodge at Alta said that in the flat light he didn't even realize he was moving until ɪт happened. And do buy your yellows ahead of time so that on the first snowy day of your ski season you don't have to waste an hour fighting the crowd in the ski shop to try to get a last-minute pair.

You can buy some glasses and goggles that have interchangeable lenses of dark for sunny and yellow for cloudy. But I like separate pairs, because I prefer glasses for sunshine and goggles for bad weather. Goggles do a better job of keeping the wind and the snow out, although they do tend to fog up unless they have some kind of ventilating system. There are another couple of reasons why I like goggles—one is psychological and the other is phony. Psychologically I like them because you feel safer when you're skiing behind them—it's almost as if you were enclosed in a protective shell where no ill could befall you. The phony is that goggles make you look fabulously pro, especially when you're sitting on the sundeck with them pushed up to your hairline or when you've taken them off and have them slipped onto your upper sleeve.

At Alta everybody claims the best goggles made are Smith goggles. These are a limited-porduction item invented by a deep-powder hound with the alias-sounding name of Bob Smith. These goggles operate on the two-layer storm-window principle and hence don't fog up in the usual way. Although they were mainly designed for deep-powder addicts, they would be of advantage to any skier out in a snowstorm. After all, even if you're only snowplowing, you need to see where you're going—maybe even more than an expert who can make last-second adjustments when he hits some unseen bump or trough.

There are two sad things about these goggles. The first is their fragility—and they don't come with a case—and the second is their price—twenty dollars. I have heard, however, that each year their design is improved so that they become more durable. By the time you read this they will probably have sturdied up to the point that they'll last you more than one season. The price, however, is not likely to drop. So if you have only one twenty-dollar bill to spend for luxuries, I'd go for the down mittens first. But if you have two twenty-dollar bills or an unlimited supply of them, by all means indulge yourself.

Face Guck

With all the elements bashing at your face you really need to put something on to keep from looking afterward as if you were one of the Mt. Rushmore four. The stuff that keeps *everything* out is zinc oxide, but if you have a face full of that you look horrible enough to frighten a grizzly, especially because it makes your teeth look yellow and ghastly. The only time you should consider using it is if you're staying away from work on sick leave to go skiing and consequently have to return looking as worm-white as you did when you left. The one person I've ever seen who looks good in zinc oxide is Stein Eriksen, but then, what doesn't he look good in? And anyway he only wears it on and around his lips.

If you burn easily and yet don't want to be an object of horror, then you can use A-Fil or Uval. A-Fil is like a heavy makeup and from a distance you look as if you have nothing at all on. Up close, if it is smeared on thick, it makes women look like decaying harlots and men somewhat worse, but no preparation is perfect and it beats scaling off your top layer of skin later. Uval disappears nicely, but if you have it on your lips, don't lick them or you'll feel you've been sucking an alum Life Saver.

If you tend to tan rather than to burn, you can use any suntan cream or lotion or oil you normally do, only use twice as much and put it on twice as often. Personally, I like to ski in something oily like Bonnie Bell's High Altitude cream simply because I think a skier looks good with a shiny face. This oily skin surface is a practical necessity if you're skiing in a snowstorm, because it keeps the snow from sticking to your face and making you resemble a Smith Brother or a retired House of David shortstop. A young ski instructor (male) with a complexion smooth enough to make an English schoolgirl envious recommended apricot oil for this anti-snow-sticking purpose, as well as for toning up before and after skiing. Apricot oil is available at health-food stores. And although the instructor assured me he was no health-food nut (and I could see he wasn't from the starchy lunch he was stowing away), he was impressed by the fact that apricot oil was one of the mainstays of the Hunzas, that high Himalayan tribe notable for their longevity (often they hit 100 plus) and their remarkable geriatric procreative abilities (eighty-year-old fathers of infants are commonplace in Hunza). Now, I don't know if these Hunzas drink the stuff or bathe in it or mainline it, but if apricot oil can do all that for them, however it's used, surely it can keep a few sun-induced squint and frown lines off our faces.

But whatever you decide to use, don't forget to put some on your ears if they hang out in the open. Sunburned earlobes sound like a joke until you have them.

Nemesis of All Evil

Finally, for good luck I recommend that somewhere on your person you carry an Ullr medal. Ullr is the Norse god of skiing. Why carry one? Well, as Dylan Thomas said in the introduction to his *Collected Poems*, "I read somewhere of a shepherd who, when asked why he made from within fairy rings ritual observances to the moon to protect his flocks, replied, 'I'd be a damn fool if I didn't!' "

Where or When

The Rodgers and Hart song "Where or When" is a musical tribute to *déjà vu*, that feeling we get of having already experienced an experience or seen a place before, when we know for sure we haven't. Reading a brochure about a ski resort and then going to the resort, you often get the opposite sensation. You might call it *jamais vu*, because the place itself often in no way resembles the multicolored, all-things-to-all-skiers promotional promises with

151

which you've filled your mind and imagination. A case in point is this enticing bit of advertising literature from:

MT. BROCHURE

Come to lovely Mt. Brochure,
  The peak of skiing pleasure,
No matter what you seek you're sure
  To find here in full measure.

An unpretentious family place,
  A playground for jet-setters,
A haven for athletes who race
  And bunnies in tight sweaters.

The snow is always fresh and new,
  The sun is ever blazing,
The action swings the whole night through,
  And the quiet is amazing.

Our runs are all steep expert class.
  Beginners just *adore* them,
And middle skiers flock en masse;
  Our slopes don't scare or bore them.

A powder hound? Then you'll be charmed,
    It's deep, dry and untracked here.
(But if you're not, don't be alarmed,
  Each flake is rolled and packed here.)

The world's most popular resort,
  The "in" place tried and tested,
Yet our lift lines are always short,
  And our slopes uncongested.

Yes, Mt. Brochure's a Wonderland,
  Come ski, relax, and caper,
It's flawless, perfect, ideal and . . .
  It just exists on paper.

Not that I'm knocking brochures. I love them. They are to me like the mail-order catalogs, or "wish books," that I spent many happy hours with as a child. I pore over my brochure collection on fall evenings, salivating and selecting a week here, a week there, picking lodges, imagining runs. I recommend that you, too, lay in a good supply of brochures of possible areas and, what the heck, a few impossible ones. You can get these by writing directly to the area or to the travel councils of the major ski states by requesting a selection from your travel agent, or, if you live in a community where there's a ski show, by going there and grabbing one of everything they're giving away.

WHERE

Reading the Resorts

Since brochures do present only the bright side, it's wise to also read up on resorts in ski magazines and in one or more of the books listed in the appendix. These describe in detail the various resorts and their accommodations and make at least some slight stab at objectivity. Even in magazine articles and books, though, the positives are always emphasized. Although I did once see a piece that put the Playboy Mt. Geneva resort through the meat-grinder, you almost never find a knocking article in a ski magazine. The obvious why is that ski magazines depend on advertising for the largest portion of their revenue, and they're not likely to bite the hand that helps them onto the financial chair lift. Then, too, since a lot of the resort guidebooks are composed of collections of articles previously published in ski magazines, the same thing holds true for them.

So since you're not likely to be reading condemnatory lines about a resort, what you're going to have to do is learn to read between the praiseful ones. You can assume that the writer is going to mention all the good points of the area. Contrariwise, you can assume that whatever is not mentioned—be it the after-ski life, the reliability of the snow conditions, the qualifications of the ski-school instructors, the comfort of the lodges—is lacking or is only minimally satisfactory. If that particular feature is an important one to your skiing happiness, then you'd be better off seeking out a resort where it *is* mentioned and praised.

A good method of verifying and checking on what you read is to grill friends and even casual acquaintances and utter strangers who have already been to the place you're considering. If I find someone who has been to an area that I haven't, I fasten myself onto him like a leech and suck out every last bloody drop of information. Often some little fact of the resort a person who has been there mentions to me turns out to be the deciding factor on whether or not I choose to go to that one.

I'd Not Walk a Mile for a Ski Lift

One thing that I personally look for as a particularly pleasant feature in a resort is being able to walk—or better still, ski—to the lifts from your lodge. That way you don't have to wrestle the car out every morning or tie yourself to the shuttle bus schedule or depend upon the kindness of strangers and in general throw away your time and energy. Of course, when I say walk, I mean a reasonable walk and not a mile hike, which can seem like a ten-mile one when you're sorely burdened with boots on your feet and skis on your shoulder.

Naturally, in many areas all the lodges are right at the bottom of the lifts—Taos and Vail spring to mind—but in others like, say, Park City, some places are within walking or skiing distance to the lifts and others are not. Usually a casual study of the resort map of the area will reveal which are which. But there's an even easier way. If you write for brochures from all the lodges and motels in the area, you can be sure that if such is the case they will have printed on them in letters only slightly smaller than their name, "SKI TO YOUR DOOR" or "ONLY 1 MINUTE TO LIFTS."

Although lift accessibility is an important consideration, sometimes the area remains well worth a stay, even if it isn't possible. Yosemite National Park's Badger Pass is an example. The nearest place to stay is eighteen miles away from Badger Pass in the Yosemite Valley. But what a place to stay! It's one of the most beautiful spots on the planet in winter—the crystallized falls scattering into giant ice punch bowls, the trees woolly with snow, the panhandling raccoons and deer brazenly demanding a forbidden handout, and Half Dome and El Capitan easily surveying the scene through clear air. It's a total delight and well worth the daily drive. So that's what you have to do: balance off the advantages, and if you have something like the Yosemite Valley or the offer of a friend's free chalet to tip the scales in favor of driving, don't sweat it. All other things being equal, though, the closer the better.

Far From the Madding Crowd

Most of the crowd-avoidance techniques will come later in the when of it, but the where can also be influential and should be considered when you make your resort selection. If you choose one far from any major population center, it stands to reason that gangs of weekenders or afternooners are not going to be clotting up the place. Take Sun Valley. They boast that the weekends there are the *least* crowded time. And it's true. Most of the one-week and two-week stayers arrive and depart on either Saturday or Sunday, so not so many of them are out skiing, and Ketchum with its total population of around 800 is not likely to contribute much toward lengthening the lift lines.

Occasionally you can choose an area close to a major city but still not horribly overrun. The resorts around Salt Lake City are good examples of this. Although Salt Lake City is a fair-sized town, the citizens have eight (8!) different ski areas within easy driving distance. They spread themselves so thin that you hardly notice they're there.

On the other hand, a place like Mammoth Mountain in California is a good five hours by well-tuned Porsche from the closest city of any size, Los Angeles. But except in rare good winters when the San Bernardino and Angelus National Forest areas are in full operation, there's no place

closer for extremely enthusiastic *Wintersportlers* of Southern California, who incidentally are so car-oriented they
think no more of driving for five hours than normal people
think of driving five minutes. You can imagine that the
slopes of Mammoth are not as deserted as their location on
the map might indicate.

Runs for the Bunny

We just-a-little-bit skiers have our own special problems in selecting a place to go. Not only do we want all the resort features our life styles require, but we also want a good assortment of easy runs which will neither scare us to death nor bore us to death. Furthermore, we want runs that give us a good measure of dignity when we ski. That is to say, we cannot be happy, no matter what else an area offers, if the only run upon which we can ski comfortably is a small, semiflat open space at the bottom of the hill served by a degrading rope tow.

No, what we want and need are a few runs up and intermingled with the intermediate and advanced runs to which we can ride on the same gondola or chairs or platter pulls or T-bars as the big kids use. We want runs that are high enough to have beautiful views and good snow and varied enough with curves and bowls and trails through the trees to let us try out the different aspects of our admittedly limited techniques. And yet we definitely do not want a beginner run that has, when we suddenly round a bend, an unexpected stretch of steep, mogully, intermediate terrain to negotiate before we're home safe. We admittedly want a lot, but if we look carefully we can find it, and we definitely should spend the time to look carefully. After all, a ski vacation is a formidable investment and we want the return on it to be pure pleasure.

I must here in all honesty modestly reveal that I am one of the world's greatest connoisseurs of easy runs. I realize that to a serious skier this claim is akin to boasting to a wine expert that you are a famed Kool-Aid taster, but nonetheless beginner runs are my bag, and I take pride in my vast knowledge of them. Naturally, in my time I have made mistakes. But more and more my beginner's dowsing rod is pointing out deep wells of just-a-little-bit-skiing contentment. So I am going to reveal to you now the cues and clues that I have learned to watch for, and that you should watch for, too.

A Track Is Not a Run

Beware of resorts advertising something like a two-and-a-half-mile beginner run, if they don't mention or show anywhere else on their run map another easy area or two. Do you know what this two-and-a-half-mile beginner run is likely, in fact almost certain, to be? A cat track. A cat track is the route the snow cat takes up the mountain and down again. A cat track is not wide enough for you to do anything but a rigid snowplow all the way down. Also, the cat track is probably so hard packed that even edging for all you're worth you'll still feel your skis are going to lose their grip and send you shooting off the edge. (Often these cat tracks have *very* sheer drops off the side.)

If this highly touted two-and-a-half-mile beginner run isn't a cat track, then it's a trail. A trail is even worse, because it is narrower and twistier and harder to negotiate than a cat track. Although an expert can do a wedeln or short swing down such trails with easy élan, for us just-a-little-bitters, skiing a long narrow trail is less fun than not skiing at all. About very few ski runs can you make that statement.

Monsters with Hearts of Gold

Do not necessarily avoid an area with an awesomely fierce reputation. Alta and Jackson Hole are good examples of this. When a just-a-little-bit skier hears harrowing tales of their fantastic vertical drops and their over-the-earlobe powder, he blanches white as the snow and quickly pushes the idea of a vacation there out of his mind.

But look again at the map of the runs. Both Alta and Jackson have separate but mercifully *not* equal and *not* fearsome hills appropriate for us just-a-little-bit types—Albion at Alta and Après Vous at Jackson Hole. On these hills, which, incidentally, are big and varied enough to be mini-resorts in themselves, a non-expert can happily mosey around the several different runs available, most of which are packed for easy skiing.

An additional advantage to such an arrangement is that at these places the hotshots are off hot-shooting the "big mountain" so you don't have to worry about them, and vice versa. For this reason places like Alta and Jackson Hole are good spots for ski trips when some of the members of the party are practically pros and the others are hardly out of the snowplow stage. With a hard and an easy mountain to choose from, no member of the group has to be bored and no member has to be in constant terror.

A final plus for going to certain well-selected "ferocious" areas is that your fellow inepters have probably been scared off and you will have the easy runs pretty much to yourself. Should you elect to take a class lesson on the lower-skill levels, it may be so small as to be semiprivate for the price of a class.

Seek the Chic

Extremely stylish resorts (for example, Sun Valley and Snowmass) almost always have a good selection of easy runs. This is because, although some of the old first family

sorts *may* have gone to school in Switzerland and consequently ski as well as they sit a horse, most of the chics on
the current market are *nouveau chic*. They have come to
ski mainly because it's the "in" thing to do. They have
come to ski and be seen, with the emphasis on the latter.
When they do ski, they want to do it without strain and
yet on runs that are as lovely and well served with lifts as
anybody is skiing on. And since these beautiful people will
happily pay beautiful prices, the ski-resort owner, like
Dickens' Barkis, "is willin'" to provide the facilities.

Skiing the runs in these high-style resorts will make you
feel very good about yourself as a skier, if not as a fashion
plate. Incidentally, although there may be a lot of super-
chics in attendance at the resort, the easy runs probably
won't be all that crowded, since this kind of skier is usually
not the dawn-to-dusk, *piste*-bashing variety. They do a lot
of deck sitting and leisurely dining and ascot tying and
other time-consuming activities that keep them off the
slopes.

Good Things Don't Always Come in Small Packages

Small areas are not always good for beginners. Just because an area has few runs doesn't mean that they're easy
runs. For example, in the little necklace of resorts around
the northern edge of the Los Angeles Basin there is one
that has only one chair and a couple of rope tows (usually
buried, if there is snow, or more commonly lying on the
bare ground). The rope-tow runs are so flat you have to
push with your poles even to move, while the chair serves
runs so steep you wouldn't want to sidestep down one
without wearing a parachute externally and a pint of
brandy internally.

Go to ... I Won't Tell

Although this chapter is not meant to be a guide to specific resorts, I have an almost uncontrollable urge to tell you about a few places where I have experienced skiing-ecstasy attacks, places where I have been totally, completely, insanely happy. But shouldn't I keep my secret pockets of skiing perfection to myself? Yes, I certainly should, but not for the selfish reasons you're thinking. I should keep them to myself—and I'm going to—because I might with my chronic hyperenthusiasm influence you to go to a place that wouldn't work for you at all. Ski-resort happiness is a very personal thing. One man's peak is another man's pique.

And, anyway, as Proust said, it isn't the *place* but the *time*. Usually what makes for a perfect stay at a ski resort is not so much where you are, but peripherals, such as whom you're with, the state of your physical, emotional and financial health, the weather, the snow, the kind of wax you have on your skis, the length of the lift lines, whether or not there's a blister on your left heel, and if your underwear is too tight or itches. That's why so often you can't go home again, meaning, of course, return to the scenes of joy and find them unchanged. Naturally it's even more difficult to go home again to somebody else's home that you've never even been to in the first place.

So just as it is with your other most important skiing decision, your bindings, it's up to you also to make up your own mind about where you're going. Even so, I can't resist giving you at least a tiny where clue. One word: *West*. And lest you think this a meaningless word from a shameless regional chauvinist, I will back it up with a quote from an Easterner, Morton Lund:

"Skiing the West is as superior to the same sport in the East as to be a different thing altogether. It's like comparing tinsel to silver or sex with love: superficially alike, but in depth the difference is awesome."

WHEN

When to go is not nearly as subjective a subject as where to go. I think we can all agree that we'd prefer a time in which there did abide these three: snow, sun, and solitude . . . and the greatest of these is solitude.

Masses on the Cold, Cold Ground

I am a lover of solitude. You might call me the Greta Garbo of the slopes. When I ski I want to be alone. As a just-a-little-bit skier I like to have the whole mountain to myself for the stem-christie windup and run-out. I agree with the Japanese that the ultimate luxury in this crowded world is privacy. And I also agree with Lenin that "one would like to embrace the masses but they bite."

On the slopes they do even worse than bite. In fact, a harmless little bite would be welcome compared to the mayhem perpetrated in ski resorts by the weekend and holiday masses, especially the *young* masses.

Never Trust a Skier Under Twenty

Although the kids don't hesitate to indict the mass of middle-agers these days, I'm truly reluctant to indict skiing

youth en masse. Some of the best skiers are young people. After all, they have the bones and muscles and coordination and nerves for it. And these good young skiers pose no problem at all to us just-a-little-bit types, mainly because they're up burning the snow off the expert runs or else serving all skikind as dedicated members of the ski patrol.

But meanwhile, back on the easy runs, we find a different breed of young people—friend-taught, boyfriend-taught, self-taught or totally untaught—full of that youthful confidence that comes from not knowing how little they know. One of the main things they don't know, along with such minor things as how to turn and stop, is what it feels like to ski in control. They don't know what it feels like for the simple reason that they have never done it.

Probably I'm overreacting on this subject, but I have a built-in magnetic attraction for out-of-control junior skiers. During an Easter week at Vail, as I was picking my way down the hill in my traditional careful manner, I heard an insistent, increasingly loud sluff-scrape of skis in the back of my ear. Then came a semihysterical shout of "Lady, I'm going to get you!" As I stiffened in horror, a teenybopper crashed by on my starboard, so close her braids brushed my face.

Then there was that time on Saturday afternoon at Heavenly Valley as I was practicing my stem christies on the easiest run. Again I heard that familiar ominous sound to the rear, followed by the shriek of, *not*, mind you, "On your left" or "On your right," so I'd know where to go, but the golden words, "Look out. I can't steer!" Again, fantastically, it was a near miss as the young lady streaked by and crashed and burned in front of me, laughing with rare good mirth when her boyfriend, who had been giving her lessons, appeared to pick her up, dust her off, refasten her bindings, and send her forth again on the slopes, a weapon fully as lethal as a submachine gun.

Several times I've been hit, too, usually by boys, who apparently have better aim than the girls, or maybe there are just more of them in both number and size. One I particularly remember at Badger Pass who skied across the front of my skis, picking me off with his elbow before going into a full roll himself. After scraping the snow out of his eyes and ears, he grinned boyishly in apology, "Sorry, lady. I just don't know how to stop these things."

A salty old gal instructor once advised me on crowded weekends to ski with my poles stuck up and out behind me, the better to skewer the out-of-control ones before they got close enough to do any damage. I can't quite bring myself to do this, because I have an ingrained reluctance to make kid kabobs, although most of them seem hell-bent on producing large batches of creamed chipped adult.

What's My Line?

Probably the only reason most of us manage to survive a weekend or holiday ski trip is that during so little of it are we actually skiing. You have to spend so much time queuing up to get on a lift that it seems you are having a lift-line-standing vacation rather than a skiing vacation. My dentist's nurse told me that once when she was up at Mammoth on the Sunday between Christmas and New Year, she got in a total of *two runs* during the entire day. The rest of the time—and she put in an eight-hour day— was spent in line either buying her lift ticket or buying her lunch or waiting to utilize the restroom facilities or—and this took most of the day—waiting to get on the lift.

The lines are so long at these times that you begin to feel that you're getting farther away from the lift rather than closer. Often this is not just a feeling but a fact. Children and teen-agers are very adept at the ancient and dishonorable art known as "taking cutsies." Either their friends or their parents slide them in or, especially in the case of smaller children, with an expression of bland innocence they just skid up to the front of the line and push onto the lift immediately. It takes a very secure adult to chew out such a cherub and send him to the end of the line where he belongs, so he usually gets away with it.

Yet the depressing truth is that you can't even always regard your interminable lift-line standing as a safety factor. Many a broken bone has resulted from an unstoppable schuss aimed at the end of the line that gets off course and instead hits somewhere in the middle, bowling over a number of hapless innocents.

Midweek White Sales

Even if you like to live dangerously and don't mind offering yourself up as a holiday human sacrifice, you have
to consider the expense. Skiing on weekends and holidays,
you definitely don't get your money's worth. Take the
dental assistant at Mammoth. With lift tickets there at
eight dollars a copy, the two runs cost her four dollars each
and while skiing is a wonderful sport, four dollars a run
does seem a bit much.

Not only do you get more for your money in midweek,
non-holiday periods, but you get more for less money.
Most resorts have bargain special midweek packages that
are a 10 or 15 or even 20 percent saving on lifts and lodg-
ings and lessons. Naturally, during Christmas and Easter
weeks, these packages are not offered and, of course, you
always pay the top dollar on weekends. You can't blame
the resort operators for this. They have to make their hay
when the crowds come. Let them. You come in the times
when it seems the whole area is being run for your private
pleasure.

Help Stamp Out Summer Vacation

The ideal way to make the ski scene when the price and
the privacy are right, instead of trying to scrunch your
snow time in on weekends and holidays, is to take your
two- or three-week annual vacation, or at least part of it,
in winter instead of in the classic—and trite—summertime.
The trick to enjoy any recreation on this overpopulated
planet is, whenever you can arrange it, to work when

others play and play when others work. A winter vacation is a good start on this program.

The one man in America who has what I consider the ideal summer/winter setup is Dr. Sam Southwick, of Jackson Hole deep-powder fame. He shares his practice in Newport Beach, California, with a yachting enthusiast. His partner is off all summer, when the sailing is easy, and Dr. Sam gets the whole winter off for his very own to do with as he pleases, and we all know what that is.

Even if you can't get absolute perfection like this, you can come very close with one, two, or three near-perfect weeks selected with care.

School Holidaze

It's not a simple matter to avoid school holidays and vacations, especially if you're going out of state on your ski trip. Schools are out of session at all kinds of weird times these days. Some colleges still operate on the standard two-semester plan, others have gone onto the quarter or trimester plan, and the breaks for all of these fall at different times. Public schools and parochial schools have their own holiday patterns, and not only do they vary from one to the other but also from state to state. It takes a heap o' letter writing to make your holiday a holiday from school holidays, but it's worth it. It will help you avoid what happened to me once: a trip to Squaw Valley on a week that coincided with the mid-semester break at Berkeley, Stanford, all of the California state colleges, and the University of Nevada. The whole place was buried under a six-foot blanket of college students seeking quick release from academic suffering. I still shudder and twitch at the remembrance.

So when you've decided where you want to go, write the public school system, the parochial diocese, and the major colleges in that state and in bordering states. Then make yourself a chart showing when the kids are all locked up and choose your week or weeks accordingly.

Another warning: When you chart your vacation remember to avoid the times around Washington's and Lincoln's birthdays. Sometimes these can be as bad or worse than Christmas and Easter.

Family Planning

What, you may ask, should you do if you have kids yourself and you want to take them skiing with you? Won't you then for sure have to fight the youth pack on the slopes? Maybe not. If you live in, say, New Jersey, you may be able to find a non-school-holiday period in Colorado or New Mexico or Utah or Canada or Idaho that fits in with your kids' days off.

And then again you may not, especially where Christmas and Easter vacations are concerned. In that case the choice is simple. Take your children out of school for a week. It's as a teacher said to a friend of mine who hesitantly asked if she thought it would be all right to take her child on a non-holiday-period ski trip. "Don't worry about it. One week of school missed isn't any great loss, especially when you compare it with the benefits he'll get from the closeness of a wonderful family ski vacation." If you're nervous about the academics of it, you can always drag along their books and assignments. Ernie Blake, of Taos, who has the right idea about a lot of things, even has a fully accredited teacher in attendance to put the kids through their school lessons in between their ski-school lessons.

Besides the immeasurable emotional good a sneaked-away week with the family will give to the children, there is some physical good. I don't mean just the exercise, which is, of course, beneficial. I mean the smaller likelihood of injury. After all, great masses of kids do bash other kids on the slopes, too. They don't just aim for adults.

These Times Were Made for Skiing

If you want to be the most alone possible on the slopes, there are two times that I consider ideal. My number one favorite is the January week immediately after Christmas vacation is over. People have usually used up all their time and money and energy during the holidays and they're ready to settle back behind the grindstone for a while. Snow is usually good and plentiful then. Rates are lower. Some places even have a special that's more special than the normal special. Instructors and lift operators and the lodge personnel are relaxed and happy knowing they've survived the Christmas crush.

The other good time to avoid the crowds only works if it's a good early-snowfall year, and even then you'll probably have to go someplace like California's Mammoth Mountain, which is famous for grabbing off the first flakes. This time is the period after Thanksgiving up to two weeks before Christmas vacation. (One week before Christmas vacation you can get involved with the quarter break at several Western colleges, as I did that time at Squaw.) An added dividend with these two periods is that you can probably wait and see how the snow is, and if it's good, you can decide to go at the last minute and still find room at the inn. For school holiday periods, especially Christmas at major resorts, you may have to book your rooms as long as two years ahead. Even for many popular (especially February) non-holiday periods at the big ones it's a matter of six months to a year. But with the really off-off-season times like these two, however, you can still manage to keep a little spontaneity in your ski life.

Snow Reports Without Snow Jobs

Most of the time your week-long vacations will have to be planned so far in advance that it's a matter of luck whether you have fresh powder or bare rocks. But if you are ever lucky enough to be able to decide on a last-minute trip based on snow conditions, there's only one way to check them out: call up the resort and ask. Snow reports collected by ski shops and airlines and newspapers are not so much dishonest or inaccurate as they are out of date. With anything as changeable as mountain weather, yesterday's packed powder may be today's rained-on slush pool. And it can work the other way around. You might decide not to go because of a poor snow report in the local paper, when at the very moment a foot of fresh fluff is falling.

Whom to call? I'd call one of the largest lodges in the area where there's a minion on duty at all hours. Naturally, if you're an old, loyal, high-tipping customer, you'll get a straight answer immediately. But even if you're not, you can learn the truth by structuring your question this way:

LODGE: Wunderbarschloss. Good evening.

YOU: Hello, who is this?

LODGE: Othmar Jones.

YOU: Oh, hi there, Othmar. How's the boy? Say, Othmar, I've been thinking I might run up there for the week if the snow's worth it. What do *you* think?

This way Othmar probably thinks he knows you or at least he thinks *you* know *him*. If you go up on his advice and he hasn't given you an accurate picture, he's likely to get at best a negative financial expression of your displeasure with him and at worst—well, who can say what a snowless skier in the throes of cabin fever might do?

April Snow

There is something to be said not just for skiing in the spring, but for taking up skiing for the first time in the spring. That something is sunshine. In the spring the weather is much more benign and not quite so intimidating as a blizzard is to fumble around in for the beginning basics. And eliminating the fear of freezing to death—or, more likely, frostbite—from your extensive collection of fears has to be helpful.

With any luck at all in the spring you'll be able to manage with only a lightweight parka and gloves or mittens. You'll be able to postpone the huge opening outlay for clothes. On top of that, whatever you do buy, either in the equipment or clothing line, you can probably get at bargain price during the end-of-the-season clearance sales.

Resort prices also hit rock bottom in the spring around the time when the snow begins to do the same. And the crowds become smaller, as many a young skier's fancy lightly turns to thoughts of surf.

There are, however, a couple of not-so-good things about spring skiing. The first is ice. It is not nice. At least, I don't think so. Some Easterners I know swear by it—instead of at it—but then they're probably making a virtue of a necessity. There is nothing in my lexicon of skiing unpleasantries to equal turning off the top of a mogul and discovering, as your skis shoot out sideways from beneath you, that it has an icy back. Nothing to equal it, of course, except riding to the top of the lift early some spring morning and discovering that the entire mountain is a sheet of diamond-hard ice, filled with an enchanting network of trippable ruts plowed into the previous day's slush by hordes of sun-worshiping skiers. Naturally, trying to learn to ski on a substance upon which it's more logical to learn to skate is less than a pleasure.

The obvious solution to the spring ice problem is to not break your neck to get out on the slopes early and as a result not break your neck. Have a few extra cups of coffee and wait until the sun softens up the terrain. Even starting out later, you'll still get plenty of slope time in, especially as a just-a-little-bit skier. Besides, later on when it's too slushy for advanced skiers' taste, you'll find it a pleasantly secure substance for skiing.

Still, in the spring, miracles have been known to happen. There have been sudden snowstorms that come along and drop a load of fresh powder. The next morning the sun comes out and, *voilà*, you have everything—fresh-packed powder, gorgeous weather, and, if it happens to be midweek, empty slopes. When all these perfections converge and merge, you almost feel like flinging yourself off the highest point of the lift, because you know you'd die totally happy.

This brings us to the other reason for not starting to ski in the spring. You may experience a miracle day of packed powder or some other similar, almost unbearable pleasure. You may become hopelessly addicted with your first exposure. And then you'll have to wait six, or more likely nine, months before you can ski again. This happened to one of my converts and it almost broke up our friendship.

"How could you do this to me?" she wailed. "You get me hooked just when the ski season's over. You must be a sadist."

Snow Is Always a Ball

Even if your life schedule is such that you have to ski with the crowds on weekends and holidays, even if there's a blizzard raging, or even if the whole mountain is encapsulated in ice, still it's better than not skiing at all. Once again, skiing is like sex. When it's great, it's fantastic, and even when it's not so hot, it's still pretty good.

I remember arriving at Badger Pass one morning in early winter when the snow was so sparse it barely covered the rocks on the runs. I spied Bernard, the French instructor I had had the previous season, and asked him, "How's the skiing?" making a face to indicate my own opinion of it. He cut me down with a stern "Whenever you can ski at all, it is good," and he skated off to the lift, whistling. When I fastened on my skis and, avoiding the bare patches, started slipping across the thin snow, a euphoric feeling suddenly swept over me and I couldn't help but agree with Bernard. Whenever you can ski, it *is* good.

Midst Alien Corn:
Skiing the Alps

It has the best-groomed of slopes and it has the worst-groomed of slopes. It has the best of skiers and it has the worst of skiers. It has the best of accommodations and it has the worst of accommodations. But if you, as a just-a-little-bit skier, go there and if you select your area with a

175

little bit of care, you are guaranteed to have only the best of times, because European skiing is our kind of skiing in every way.

Synergistic, Symbiotic Synthesis

A ski trip and a European tour make a synergistic, symbiotic synthesis. It's synergistic, because the pleasure you derive from the combination is greater than the sum total of the pleasure of each part. It's symbiotic, because a ski trip and a European tour live together in a mutually beneficial way. Being in Europe makes a ski trip better, and skiing makes a European tour better. This is because you are instantly relieved of the traditional compulsives of both skiing and touring.

Look at it this way. If you are all the way over there in Europe, you won't feel guilty if you don't spend every minute of every day out there on the slopes perfecting your whatever. After all, this is a European trip. You ought to have some time to poke around the shops and *Weinstuben* and coffeehouses in the villages and experience the foreign experience. You'd be in idiot not to. So if the day is stormy or the slopes are icy or for some reason or other you just don't feel like skiing (it *does* happen sometimes to the best of fanatics), you don't fight it. You just relax and enjoy yourself.

And yet, and yet, it *is* a ski trip, so you have to spend some of your time on the slopes. And this, in turn, relieves you of all that grim sightseeing you ordinarily feel compelled to do on a European trip. Besides that, the Alps are not long on such obligatory sights as museums and cathedrals and opera houses and châteaux. Their major tourist attractions are of the outdoor variety, the kind you can see best from the top of a lift or a mountain-peak restaurant, of which there are so many.

Also, you *can't* tour around too much. Not only is time a problem if you're going to ski, but in the major resorts usually you have to book your hotel for a minimum of a week's stay. So you are condemned to slow down and, here we go again, just relax and enjoy yourself.

Ski as the Romans Do

There's still another something that makes it possible for us just-a-little-bit skiers to relax and enjoy ourselves in Europe. That's our companions on the slopes. In America you find a preponderance of good, strong intermediate skiers slaving to become experts, the kind Ernie Blake refers to as "those dreadfully ambitious American skiers." When you're home in ambitionland, it's hard even for the most dedicated just-a-little-bit type not to feel a twinge of shame if he's not out there flailing himself on the slopes for eight hours a day the way his fellow countrymen are.

This is not true in Europe. You do not find so many strong intermediates. There, almost everyone is either magnificent or terrible. When Europeans are good, they are very, very good, and when they are bad, they are lousy. The only explanation I have for this phenomenon is that if a European lives in or near a ski resort he's probably skied so much that it's second, or maybe even first, nature to him. And if he's all that good, he's probably a racer or an instructor or officially connected with the ski or resort business in some way. While if the European is a city dweller or a Johann or Jean or Giovanni-come-lately to skiing, he doesn't have the desperate Puritan ethic desire that Americans have to turn their vacations into work. He's able to make skiing what it should be—play.

When a European has a ski holiday, the emphasis is on the holiday rather than on the ski. Many Europeans consider it a tremendous accomplishment to do two runs a day. And so it is, what with sleeping until ten o'clock and having a leisurely breakfast followed shortly afterward by a leisurely mid-morning coffee and then an even more leisurely lunch (around two hours) with a postprandial sundeck sit. Then comes the afternoon tea combined with dancing, which takes care of another couple of hours. Naturally, one needs a bit of rest before dinner and some music and song and wine after dinner before toddling off to bolster and down comforter.

Haute Haute Cuisine

In Alpine resorts eating is a big thing. It is definitely not, as a Jackson Hole ski and mountaineering instructor referred to American resort food, "a cheese sandwich and forget it." Even if you did decide to just get by on a cheese sandwich in the Alps, you definitely wouldn't forget it, because you'd probably make it yourself with a chewy, crusty loaf you picked up in the bakery and a hunk of some delightful regional cheese like Emmenthaler, and all would slip down on ripples of a liquid regional, one of the "little" wines that aren't exported, such as the Swiss Dôle or the Austrian Kalterersee or the French Crépey.

Generally, however, you'll follow the European way of eating a many-coursed repast of delectables. Which brings us to another compatibility between European tours and ski trips. You *can* stow away the magnificent meals without anguishing over your calorie counter, because you won't be spending your time sitting in a tour bus fattening up. No, you'll soon be off on the slopes working it off at the rate of six hundred to seven hundred calories an hour.

Playing the Numbers

OK, so now I've convinced you that you should ski the Alps. Now how am I going to convince you that you can afford it? Simple. I will show you some statistics I have compiled. As Mark Twain said, "There are three kinds of lies: lies, damned lies, and statistics." To prove that I'm not

lying I'll admit that if you are comparing a trip to the Alps with a day trip to a local area within driving distance of your home, there is no comparison. Mt. Blanc would tower above Mt. Minuscule as much in price as it does in meters. But if you are considering a two- or three-week vacation at a major U.S. resort to which you would have to fly, you can do as well or better going to Europe, especially if you are an Easterner.

Even if you are, like me, a Westerner from about as far west as you can get, you can still make it. Just read this letter which I sent to a couple of West Coast friends whom I was trying to con into joining me on a charter flight to Europe rather than going to a well-known American resort, which I shall here call Nameless-at-Anonymous, so as not to offend.

DEAR TRAVEL COMPANIONS:

Can you believe this? I hardly can myself. Three weeks in Nameless-at-Anonymous, including the same sort of everything, would cost $97.27 *more* than three weeks in Europe. Of course, you could logically say you wouldn't spend three weeks in Nameless—and well you might not, because you would frost over with boredom if you did. There is nothing to do there but ski, while Europe (five countries) is a constant succession of delights.

Startling though these figures may seem, they still do not tell the whole story. In order to be totally fair and not misrepresent anything to you I have bent over backwards to give Nameless-at-Anonymous the advantages of cost. I have, in fact, been *unfair* to Europe. For example, I have said that lunch in Lech would be two dollars a person and in Nameless one dollar and fifty cents. In reality, since Austria is one of the cheapest countries in the world and the U. S. one of the most expensive, it would probably be the other way around and then some. Also, you probably would pay more than twenty-two dollars for your Nameless-at-Anonymous room, while you will probably pay less than the prices listed for hotels in Munich, Milano, and Geneva. Not only that, but taxes and services (tips) are included in the European rates, while they are not in the Nameless-at-Anonymous rate.

And remember, the meals you will have in Europe, especially at the *Guide Michelin* two-star restaurants and at Courchevel, where the hotel restaurant is a one-star, will be as close to dining perfection as you can find on this planet, while those at Nameless will be pretty much standard American. True, there are a couple of exotic dining spots over in Anonymous, but if you decide to indulge in them, you should up the dinner charge to at least twenty to twenty-five dollars, and the food will still not be within yodeling distance of what you'll have in Europe.

Top all this off with the utterly delightful companion you'll have on the European trip, and it would seem that logic would dictate that there is no choice. It *must* be Europe.

European Ski Trip Expenses for Two Persons
(Munich-Lech-Madonna di Campiglio-Courchevel-Geneva)

Charter flight (all meals & *drinks* included) . . .	590.00
Munich hotel (2 nights)	30.00
Munich meals (2 days)	20.00
Meals Munich-Lech en route	10.00
Lech hotel (4 nights demi-pension)	78.00
Extra meals in Lech (4 lunches)	16.00
Lunch Innsbruck-Madonna di Campiglio en route . .	4.00
Madonna di Campiglio hotel (4 nights full pension) .	122.00
Lunch in Verona (Guide Michelin ** restaurant) . .	11.00
Milan hotel (1 night)	17.00
Dinner in Milan (Guide Michelin ** restaurant) . .	14.00
Lunch in Chamonix or Megève (Guide Michelin	
* restaurant)	12.00
Courchevel hotel (7 nights full pension)	224.00
Geneva hotel (1 night)	20.00
Meals in Geneva (2 lunches, 1 dinner)	27.00
Misc. snacks	75.00
Misc. booze	75.00
Lift tickets	
1 week Courchevel	70.00
All other areas—coupon books	50.00
Tips	50.00
VW for 3 weeks including mileage and gas	200.00
Total **$1715.00**	

NOTE: These estimates are extremely generous. For example, as far as the extra meals are concerned, the wine would probably be included in the estimated price, hence the $75.00 for Misc. booze would be only for wine with meals where on pension, and any occasional glasses consumed. Also, can you eat $75.00 worth of Misc. snacks?

Nameless-at-Anonymous Ski Trip Expenses for Two Persons

Air tickets (about $73.50 each, *if* you can fit yourself
   into the excursion-fare schedule;
   otherwise over $90.00) 147.00
Transporting of skis on air flight
   (it's free on the European charter) 12.00
Hotel ($22.00) 462.00
Breakfasts ($2.00 each) 84.00
Lunches ($1.50 each) 63.00
Dinners ($15.00 for two) 315.00
Misc. snacks 75.00
Misc. booze 75.00
Lift tickets ($7.50 each) 315.00
Automobile rental (cheapest available model) . . . 264.27
Total $1812.27

Charter Your Course

Naturally, my cool logic won them over. How about you? Of course, I'll admit that for a West Coast resident a crucial item is the air fare, and to make the figures come out as well as this, you would need to be on a charter, but that's not hard to do in these days of so many quasi-phony "international friendship" organizations founded mainly to aid and abet people who are looking for bargain air fares to Europe.

There are also a lot of non-phony organizations that do other things besides have charter flights, and frankly I advise hooking up with one of those. The government is starting to crack down on the quasi-phonies and you just might find yourself at the last minute all packed up with no plane to go on.

A clue I've found to indicate a more legitimate outfit is that they usually fly their charters with the major scheduled airlines rather than the supplemental carriers. Another clue is that they are always more meticulous than a Supreme Court justice when it comes to the letter of the law. For example, I wanted to mention here a most legitimate ski-oriented organization that did chartering of European flights along with myriads of other things beneficial for skiing and skiers. But they screamed like minks at the idea because it smacked of "advertising charter flights," which is strictly against the rules. So you'll just have to poke around and find your own organization—but remember, do your charter shopping early because you have to be a member at least six months before the date of the flight.

Frankly, I prefer charters for ski trips, because you get to take sixty-six pounds of luggage instead of the forty-four pounds allowed on regular flights. That's important. Enough winter clothing for two or three weeks in Europe is not light, and ski equipment is just as heavy in an airplane hold as it feels on you at the end of a day on the slopes.

The only hazard of a charter air flight—aside from the fact that you travel in an airplane—is that if you become ill or, dare I say it?, break something overseas, you would need to fly home fast, and this would steam-roller your travel budget, since you get no refund on unused charter flights, and a one-way scheduled flight home usually costs more than the round-trip charter price. You can easily protect yourself from this eventuality now by purchasing what is called an air-fare protector policy. For three hundred dollars' worth of coverage, this will cost only seven dollars and fifty cents and can be obtained through the travel agent handling the charter for the organization.

GIT Along Little Skier

GIT stands for Group Inclusive Tours, and they are not a bad second-best thrift choice for you if you can't fit yourself onto a charter. On one of these you fly on a regular scheduled flight on a regular scheduled airline with a group of at least fifteen people. Don't worry about finding the group. The airlines put it together with their little computer. During the ski season there are several departures every Friday and Saturday going to the major Alpine gateway cities—Munich, Geneva, Zurich, Lyon, and Milan. Trips are available for both two- and three-week periods and you can go anywhere you want to. You are no more stuck to stick with your GIT companions after you land than you are with those on a charter. You do, of course, have to fly back with the gang. Airlines offering GIT ski flights are Air France, Austrian Airlines, BOAC, Lufthansa, Pan American, Swissair and TWA.

The only other stipulation in this deal is that you have to purchase a certain percentage of your land arrangements (hotels, car rental, etc.) in conjunction with the tour. But unless you demand total footloosedness—and incidentally are willing as a result to curl up under a bridge when you can't find a room—this is no great disadvantage. All it means is that you must pick out the hotels you want to stay in in advance. The GIT tours have four price levels to choose from in all the major resorts.

These days arranging your hotels as a part of a GIT package can be an actual advantage. General Tours (49 West 57th Street, New York, N.Y. 10019), the organization that handles most of the GIT ski tours, has blocked out so many of the rooms in Alpine hotels for anticipated use with their tours that it's often hard for us independents to get a foot in the door. I remember I was planning to spend a few days in Lech, Austria, in February 1970, and I started writing to the hotels there in August 1969. I got nothing but turndowns, partially because I was going to stay less than a week, but also because so many of the rooms were spoken for in advance. Finally the only way I managed to find shelter from the storm was by leaving a plaintive note at the Austrian booth at the Los Angeles Ski Show for Othmar Schneider, who was appearing there and happened to own a superb little gem of a hotel in Lech. He very kindly swung open the door. Probably *he* wouldn't have had any room, either, except for the fact that his hotel, the Kristiania, had been open for only a year and hence had probably not become locked into the tourist circuit as yet.

The time I went on a GIT tour it ran as smoothly as a Swiss watch. The VW was waiting where it was supposed to be, all the flights were right on the dot and miraculously uncrowded, all the hotels were expecting us and had our prepayments in order. General Tours knows what it's doing. The only hitch in our plans came when we arrived at our hotel in Megève and found it closed—through no fault of General Tours. The chimney had developed a lethal leak and the management had closed for immediate repairs. The owner of the battened-down hotel arranged for us to stay at a hotel owned by one of his friends—a hotel in a higher category—at no additional price.

One warning on these GIT packages: that microscopically small price you see in the magazine ads—"Your very own Alp for just $295"—is, to put it politely, unrealistic. If you're a typical American, that is to say, a bathroom fetishist (and who isn't on a ski trip?), then you're not going to be happy with the cheapest, or one-star, version. You are, in fact, going to have to hop all the way up to the three-star category in order to get the private plumbing your compulsions require. But that's not too bad, because on a three-star package, along with the tub, you also get the Bug. If there are two of you traveling together, they throw in the use of a Volkswagen (you pay your own gas and mileage). A VW is, I believe, the best way to get around because you come and go when you want to instead of when the bus or train wants to, and it also makes day trips to neighboring resorts possible and easy.

Incidentally, I would consider the four-star package not only unnecessary but a detriment. The hotels are so luxurious they make you uncomfortable and so international they totally lack national character and charm.

For further facts and figures contact your travel agent, the participating airlines, or General Tours.

High at Twice the Price

If the GIT arrangement doesn't work for you, although for the life of me I can't see why it wouldn't, you can always wing it with an excursion fare. The prices and regulations on these change about every two or three days, so you'll have to check with your travel agent to see the latest Mickey Mousing on dates and times you have to go through to get the best price.

The most recent fare innovation the airlines have come up with is the "affinity group." This plan costs less than an excursion flight and even less than a GIT flight, but it has its little complications. It's something like a charter in that

you have to be part of a group of eighty or more people flying both ways together, and the airline can't make up the
group for you. It has to be made up of members of a legitimate organization—not just people who happen to want
to fly somewhere together—and you must have belonged
to the group for six or more months. As with the GIT system, you fly a regularly scheduled flight of a regularly
scheduled airline. But unlike going GIT, you don't have to
prepay any ground arrangements ahead of time.

If you have some kind of sickness that makes you want
to spend money unnecessarily, you can always just telephone an airline office and tell them when and where you
want to go and let the devil take the hindmost—and the
airline will relieve you of all the rest.

Take It Along, Take It All Along

Every learned travel writer always advises you to take
as little clothing and paraphernalia as possible on an overseas trip. True. But while keeping this age-old travel-light
rule in mind, you still should be careful to take with you
everything you'll need both for being in Europe and for
skiing in Europe. This is not because you're going to a
Siberia-like wasteland. You're not. European resorts can
supply you with everything you'll ever need. No, the point
is that to go out and purchase new items takes that one
irreplaceable life commodity—time. Since you have only
so many hours a day for being and skiing in Europe, you
shouldn't have to waste them waiting for bindings to be
mounted on new skis or trying to translate European sizes
into American ones. "Have to" are the key words here. If
you get over there and *want* to do some shopping—have
some pants tailored to your size or have some custom-

made boots cobbled out at Strolz in Lech or Molitor in Wengen or Haderer in Kitzbühel—fine. Go right ahead. But don't make your skiing or your comfort depend on being able to find a certain something immediately. In desperate cases like that you're likely *never* to find it.

Especially with ski equipment, I don't think it's a good idea to go over and buy everything new, an additional reason being that you won't be used to it. There will be enough confusions going for you, as it is—strange runs, strange customs, and strange strangers—without adding strange skis or boots or bindings to the confusion. No, keep your old reliables for skiing-security blankets. If you do buy new equipment, take it or send it home and break it in on familiar slopes.

One little hint about after-ski clothing: take to the Alps whatever you normally take on U.S. ski trips but be sure your wardrobe also includes, depending on your gender, a couple of dresses or some kind of coat-and-tie combination. In some of the higher-class dining rooms you'll feel very Ugly American if you don't dress up to the local idea of snuff.

An Alpine for the Teacher

One of the greatest of Alpine bargains is ski-school lessons. Although the cost may vary slightly, depending on the poshness of the station, in general you can figure a private lesson over there costs about the same as a class lesson in the U.S. If you go along with the basic just-a-little-bit premise of taking only private lessons after the beginning stem christie, you can see what a formidable savings this would be.

Many European ski-trip takers who are touching down

in two or three different countries worry about taking lessons from instructors of the different national schools for fear that something will be . . .

Lost in the Translation

I've had lessons from Hans, Bill, Luigi,
Pierre, Franzl, Harry and Jack,
   And I think you'll agree
   From the way that I ski,
I should ask for my money back.

Now my head and my shoulders twist Swiss style,
My waist has an Austrian bend,
   Français is my torso—
   My hands even more so—
And Italian is my living end.

Down under, my knees are Australian,
As Canadian caper my feet,
   And in total skin hue
   I'm red, white (black) and blue,
As American as you can meet.

My poor body's a U. N. Assembly
Debating an imminent fall,
   While this skier of Babel
   Stands confused and unable
To get down the hill at all.

This shouldn't be too great a worry for you, though. After all, you've probably developed pretty much of a mongrel technique already from learning from imported instructors in America. Most U.S. resorts pride themselves on quite an international selection of teachers, and although all ostensibly teach American technique, I've often noticed a strong foreign accent in more ways than one.

But if you do worry about confusions, you could do as I usually do. I take lessons in only one country, and I favor Austria. Most of the time it's the first country I go to, since the charter I generally fly with lands in Munich. The lessons are comparatively inexpensive in Austria and I like the Austrian technique. Although I understand that theoretically and in inter-ski demonstrations the Austrian school has changed to a wider track, squarer on the skis, and less angulated technique, on the practical level I've noticed that most of the oldest established, permanent skiing *skilehrers* still teach the exaggerated angulation, exaggerated counterrotation, skis-together Austrian classic style. And as I say, I like this. I like it because when you learn such a rigid technique and then go off and ski on your own in a more relaxed (sloppy) manner, you still have enough residual technique to carry you through—while if you learn a relaxed and casual technique to begin with and you slop *it* up, you may wind up with no technique at all.

But no matter what national school you elect to learn from, you're certain to come home with something beneficial from it. If nothing else, you'll have a terrific put-down ready if someone ever regards your skiing technique with a sneer of distaste and asks, "Where did you learn to ski like that?" When you answer "St. Anton" or "Cortina" or "Chamonix" or "Davos," that should end the conversation nicely.

Another advantage of the low cost of European instructors is that they can be hired as guides for all day. For three persons to have divine guidance on the slopes, it costs only a total of seventeen to twenty dollars. Having someone lead you to the best snow and the runs on your level of skiing or show you the route to take to visit neighboring villages and in general give you an overview of the possibilities of the station is a marvelous way to start your stay. You immediately feel at home and can enjoy every minute of your skiing rather than wasting time cautiously groping. Naturally, for skiing glaciers and avalanche-prone areas a guide is a must, but who among *us* is going to be doing that?

Adoring foreign instructors and lessons as I do, I still feel I should mention something an Englishman once told me. He's a pilot for Swissair on the run between Zurich and New York, and he's an avid skier whose skis have massaged the runs of every major resort in the world. He told me that of all ski instructors he prefers the Americans. He finds American instructors much more articulate in their explanations. With the European instructors, he maintains, communication is apt to be somewhat fuzzy. According to his theory, this is not just the language barrier—most of them speak fluent ski in four languages. Rather, it's that they spend their off-season time engaged in manual or agricultural pursuits. The Americans, on the other hand, are usually college students or college graduates who spend their off-the-skis time in pursuits that are more mind-honing.

Maybe so. On the other hand, I've talked to Austrian and French instructors who were not only very articulate but who expressed amazement at the small amount of training some of the American instructors get by with. Skiing is a lifelong career for them, and to earn their national ski-instructor medallion takes up to three years of hard work and requires a rigid annual test for renewal. For many American instructors, however, teaching skiing is just a youthful interlude.

As you can see, you pays your money and you takes your choice, but with the Europeans, at least, you do pay quite a bit less money.

WO? OU? DOVE?

Where is both easier and harder to decide in Europe than at home. It's easier because for some reason the guidebooks to European resorts (see appendix) are a little less hesitant about pointing out defects. Abby Rand bluntly says, for instance, that in Kitzbühel "lift lines are horrendous" and continues with the information that the riskiness of the snow often sends "Kitzbühel refugees fleeing to higher slopes." Egon Ronay doesn't hesitate to minus a resort for "no night life," "highly commercial atmosphere," "lack of parking space," and "lack of really good cafés and restaurants." Only Saul Galin remains eternally optimistic about sun and snow and run variety. I think this is because he's European, while the first two are American and English, and he's therefore more full of the old common-market spirit.

The hard part of resort selection is that there are so many to choose from—literally hundreds, if you count the minor ones, which are not so very minor by American standards. Write to the tourist bureau of each area that you are considering for brochures that will drive you mad with desire. All these resorts sound, and most actually *are*, so tremendously delectable that it's really hard to make a decision. As an old epicurean philosopher put it, there is nothing more difficult than choosing between luxuries.

You may get some help in your decision by where the plane lands and takes off. Some resorts are just too far away from others via Alpine roads to combine compatibly. As Abby Rand puts it, "The best way to get from Val d'Isère to Kitzbühel is to go home and come back again."

How many different resorts can you visit? I think that on a two-week trip you should plan on hitting only two stations and on a three-week trip three. Naturally, you *could* hit more than that, but besides knocking yourself out and wasting time in a car when you could be skiing or meandering in your village, many hotels, as I said before, are more than reluctant to book you for less than a week.

If you are, however, an incurable lecher when it comes to wanderlust, I offer you this response made by ski-movie maker Dick Barrymore to the query, "Can you pick out three, four, five areas and do them in two weeks?"

"Sure, the main thing is to avoid traveling during the days you could be skiing. Travel so you can leave your ski resort by 4:00 or 5:00 P.M. and be at your next hotel by 8:00 or 9:00 P.M. . . . In two weeks you can cover a lot of ski resorts that way."

Whew!

Heidi Tries Harder

Is there any universally recognized peak among the Alpine countries? As far as I know, none at all. Naturally, the big four are Switzerland, Austria, France and Italy. Germany has some resorts, but they are smaller or, in the case of Garmisch, pretty overcrowded, what with the combination of Germans and GIs. When it comes to making a selection, that old devil personal taste rears its head again.

If you've never been to Europe at all and feel a little nervous about the whole thing, Switzerland might be good for an opener. All surveys show Switzerland to be the miles-ahead favorite European country for ski-vacationing Americans. This is mainly, I think, because it feels the least foreign. You might call it foreign travel for people who don't like foreign travel. Everything is geared to the tourist's comfort. The Swiss are the original and best hotel-keepers. The Swiss cuisine is international with few mystery concoctions, and that travel-brochure propaganda of "Everybody speaks English" is truer in Switzerland than in any other country except perhaps Holland, and there the slopes aren't much.

Actually, if you spent your whole ski vacation in Swiss resorts, you could get a whiff of France and Italy and Austria by selecting resorts closest to their borders. You'd find that Switzerland tends to sponge up the traits of cuisine, language, and even national spirit from its neighbors.

The neighboring Alpine countries are also influenced by their proximity to Switzerland. Many Americans returning from European tours have been heard to remark, "But it was so *dirty*," as they curl up nose and lip at the remembrance of fly-incrusted beeves in a butcher shop or century-old bathtub rings. But the Italian, French, and Austrian Alpine resorts are as clean as a Swiss whistle and you *can* drink the water.

Trio Con Brio

If you've been to Europe before or if you're an adventuresome sort who doesn't mind an occasional linguistic or gastronomic contretemps, then go for the real thing and try Austria, Italy, or France instead of the diluted Swiss version. That way you'll get all the change of atmosphere that gives you the real impact of foreign travel.

Austria

The Austrians are the inventors of whipped cream and *Gemütlichkeit,* or at least, if they didn't invent them, they are the world's foremost pushers of these two highly addictive commodities. The Austrians also invented skiing, or at least, if they didn't invent it, they were the first to systematize the teaching of this highly addictive sport. All of this mind-blowing Austrian style takes place in the most living-color picture-post-card villages of Europe. Try walking down the street of Lech some night with the snow falling and the river gurgling and the bell clanging in the tower of the stone church. *Unvergesslich!*

The amazing part of it all is that attached to this prize ski package is the lowest price tag in the Alps. It is admittedly not a great deal lower than the rest, but it *is* the lowest. You can, for example, sit all night in a wine cellar listening to the zither and dancing for the price of a very cheap glass of wine, the only stipulation being that you must join in on the chorus of *"Wien, Wien, Nur Du Allein,"* which is sung approximately every quarter hour on the quarter hour.

The one fly in the delectable ointment of Austria is that

the secret is out and the more popular resorts there are so popular that you must book your rooms about a year in advance. If you can't plan that far ahead, you can always go to one of the less well-known stations. There are, after all, eighty-six to choose from.

P.S. Advantage for us just-a-little-bit types: As a general rule the mountains in Austria are less high than those of Switzerland and France. Hurrah!

France

Years ago it was said that every American has two native lands, his own and France. I agree. Even back during the De Gaulle days when it was considered high treason for an American to spend tourist dollars there, I used to sneak across the border from my "Swiss ski vacations" and have my illicit interludes with *la belle France*. As far as outgoing charm is concerned, it's true that more French come on like the irascible Marielle Goitschel than the delightful Jean-Claude Killy, but I don't feel affronted by this. After all, as a sage once remarked, "Why do you expect the French to like tourists when they don't even like each other?"

Probably the main reason I have this unseverable umbilical-cord attachment to France is the cuisine. Dining and wining in France are beyond all description and belief. As a result, in all but the swingingest resorts, the evening meal is usually the big after-ski event.

The slopes in French, as in all other European resorts, are maintained almost exclusively by "human groomin'," but in the newly developed ones, notably Courchevel and La Plagne, you couldn't find smoother surfaces this side of a pool-table factory.

France is the most expensive of all the places to go, but in my opinion it's worth every sou. Of course, my opinion is probably worthless, because I always see France through a lover's eyes, which inevitably turn *la vie en blanc* there into *la vie en rose*.

Italy

It's the least touristy of all the ski-resort countries. When you're there you definitely do *not* feel you are at Aspen East the way you do in some of the best-known Swiss, French, and Austrian stations. It's a multifaceted aesthetic experience just to be in Italy. Some call the mountains there, especially the Dolomites, the most scenic on earth, while the Italians themselves are beautiful people in both the jet-set style and the human-warmth senses of the word. And *joie de vivre* is such an Italian characteristic that it ought to be known the world around as *gioia di vivere*.

If English isn't spoken as commonly in Italy as it is in other Alpine countries—and it isn't—communication is not all that difficult. The Italians know a few words in your language; you know a few words in theirs (*prego* covers almost any situation); and the hands and eyes take care of the rest.

The night life is very whoopee and the day life of the slopes is a little like rush hour in the Piazza di Spagna, although the slopes themselves are beautifully manicured and the lift equipment looks and works as if it were put together in the Ferrari factory. The cuisine is double-surprisingly non-"typical Italian" cuisine. That is, it is *not* heavy and garlicky.

At the moment Italy is the most imaginative place to go, and you can beat the American tourist hordes there—if you hurry.

Twist Tongues, Not Knees

Another big part of the excitement of moving from country to country is the linguistic gear-shifting involved. As Dick Barrymore says, "You're crossing one border and you have to learn to say *merci* instead of *danke*. You get mixed up. And that's what is fun about it."

Using different languages *is* a lot of fun, and every phrase you can nail into your head before you go will be invaluable. You can pick up the amenities in any phrase book, and there is a list of ski terms in German, French, and Italian in the appendix in this book. But even more important are the phrases you never find in any conversation manual that are vital to just-a-little-bit-skiing needs. These are phrases directly translated from our frequently employed "Chicken English" that you will want to use with your foreign instructors and slope companions.

Chicken English

1. Does this lift go to the beginner areas? Is it hard to get off of?
2. Please tell me where the easy runs are.
3. I am not a very good skier. I can only do a rather poor stem christie (stem turn; snowplow).
4. I cannot ski ice (moguls; powder).
5. Don't take me on any difficult runs. I am one of the world's great cowards.
6. I cannot ski down this hill. It is too steep.
7. I am terrified!
8. Not so fast!
9. Stop! Help!
10. On your left; on your right.
11. Look out!
12. Mild expletive. Medium expletive. Strong expletive (not recommended for ladies when others are within earshot).
13. What did I do wrong?
14. I have twisted my knee.
15. I think I have broken my leg (ankle).
16. Is there a ski patrol here? What do they charge to take a body down the hill?*
17. Anybody want to buy a pair of skis cheap?

*Yes, Virginia (and Virgil) there is a charge in Europe for the ski-patrol service. It can run from five dollars to fifty dollars, depending on the distance the "Good Samaritans" have to go to fetch the body.

French

1. Est-ce que le monte-pente va à la piste des débutants?
2. Veuillez me dire où il y a des pentes faciles.
3. Je ne suis pas bon skieur (bonne skieuse). Je ne réussis pas encore très bien stem christiania (stem; chasse-neige).
4. Je ne peux pas skier sur la neige glacée (les bosses; la neige poudreuse).
5. Ne m'emmenez pas sur des pistes difficiles. Je suis un des plus grands froussards (une des plus grandes froussardes) du monde.
6. Je ne peux pas descendre cette pente en ski. Elle est trop raide.
7. J'ai une frousse bleue.
8. N'allez pas si vite.
9. Arrêtez-vous! Au secours!
10. À gauche; à droite.
11. Attention!
12. Mon Dieu! Zut alors! Merde!
13. Qu'est-ce que j'ai fait de mal?
14. Je me suis tordu le genou.
15. Je crois que je me suis cassé la jambe (la cheville).
16. Y a-t-il un ski patrol ici? Combien est-ce que ça coute pour descendre quelqu'un?
17. Qui veut acheter une paire de skis à très bon marché?

German

1. Geht dieser Lift zu den Anfängerhängen? Ist es schwer, auszusteigen?
2. Sagen Sie mir, bitte, wo die leichten Abhänge sind.
3. Ich bin kein guter Skiläufer (keine gute Skiläuferin). Ich kann nur Stem Christiania (Stemmbogen, Schneepflug).
4. Auf Eis (Buckel, Pulverschnee) kann ich nicht skifahren.
5. Bitte, nehmen Sie mich auf keine schwierigen Abfahrten mit. Ich bin einer der grössten Feiglinge auf der Welt.
6. Ich kann da nicht hinunterfahren; es ist zu steil.
7. Ich habe grosse Angst!
8. Nicht so Schnell!
9. Halt! Hilfe!
10. Links; Rechts.
11. Vorsicht!
12. Du liebe Zeit! Verdammt! Scheiss!
13. Was hab ich denn falsch gemacht?
14. Ich habe mein Knie verrenkt.
15. Ich glaube ich hab das Bein (Fussgelenk) gebrochen.
16. Gibt es hier eine Skipatrouille? Was kostet es, eine Leiche vom Berg herunterzuholen?
17. Wer will ganz billig ein Paar Skier kaufen?

Italian

1. Va questo "lift" alle piste dei principianti? È difficile scendere dal "lift"?
2. Potrebbe dirmi dove sono le piste più facili.
3. Io non sono un sciatore molto bravo. Appena posso fare una stem-christiania (stem, spazza neve).
4. Non posso sciare sul ghiaccio (gobbe, nella neve profonda).
5. Non mi porti nelle piste difficili. Io sono uno dei più bravi impauriti.
6. Io non posso sciare su questa montagna. È troppo ripida.
7. Sono spaventato!
8. Non andare cosi veloce!
9. Fermare! Aiuto!
10. A sinistra; a destra.
11. Attenzione!
12. Mamma mia! Maldire! Merda!
13. Cosa ho fatto di male?
14. Io mi sono slogiato il ginocchio.
15. Io penso che ho una gamba (una caviglia) rotta.
16. C'è la pattuglia dello sci qui vicino? Quanto costerebbe scendere la montagna con loro?
17. C'è qualcuno che voglia comprare a buon mercato i mie sci?

WANN? QUAND? QUANDO?

The when of the Alps is not too different from the when of the U.S. Like us, Europeans tend to blow their financial and physical resources over the end-of-the-year holidays, making the last three weeks in January their low season in both prices and crowds. Many European resorts also have special bargain rates the first two weeks of December— and some even have snow.

As you might suspect, Lincoln's and Washington's birthdays are no big thing over there, but they do fall in the February high season, again both in crowds and prices.

Because of the prevailing non-puritanical attitude toward wholehearted holidaying, Alpine resorts are usually more crowded than U.S. resorts during midweek periods. The increasing number of American skiers being pumped into Europe on ski tours doesn't help. But just because European resorts are more crowded during the midweek doesn't mean, I'm sorry to say, that they're less crowded than American ones on weekends and school holidays. It just means that weekends over there are extra-super-crowded. And the school holidays are even tougher to chart there than here. Would you believe a *vacances scolaires* in France the third week of February? I think it has something to do with the start of Lent, but whyever, I once had the misfortune to hit it head on.

The good old reliable mob scene during the two weeks around Christmas holds as true in the Alps as it does in the Rockies. Although there are a lot of charters and ski packages that make it easy and convenient for you to go at that time, I'd advise against Christmas in Europe if you have any other choice. This is not just because of the crowds. I'd mainly advise against it because since the holidays are such an innkeepers' market, they can and do refuse to book a room in a resort for anything less than two weeks. If you have only a two-week vacation, it's pretty obvious that you're only going to see one station, and while that's not bad, it's better to see more of Europe than one village if you're going to all the trouble to fly over.

If you *must* go at this time, then try to stay in a ski resort that is close enough to another one or two to permit you to ski both, while obeying the two-week rule. In Austria, if you go to either Lech, Zürs, St. Anton or St. Christoph, you could easily visit the others. In France, if you were at Val d'Isère you could pop over to Tignes; with Courchevel there's Meribel; and with Megève, Saint Gervais. In Grindelwald you're right next to Wengen and Mürren, while if you're at Zermatt, you could make it a two-country holiday with a zip trip over to Cervinia in Italy. Italy and France can also be combined with Chamonix and Courmaycur.

Don't Give Up the Alps for Lent

Although it always falls at the height of high season, it's a ski-trip highlight to indulge in the carnival period in Europe. Especially this is true in Munich, where Fasching annually fights it out with the Oktoberfest for the orgy trophy. If it fits into your schedule, you might try to land or take off in Munich. It's the most convenient gateway to the Austrian resorts. Luckily it's easy to get in on the pre-Lenten festival period in Munich, since they usually start celebrating about the time their New Year's Eve hangovers have stopped throbbing. The other countries also have a pre-Lenten wingding, but it's usually concentrated into a one-week period.

When the Hounds of Spring Are on Winter's Traces

Although the Alps are legendary cloudscrapers, not every Alp or every Alpine resort is all that high. In some areas you have to start worrying about snow conditions at the beginning of March, and in a really bad year at the end of February. You can, however, be fairly sure of finding something skiable toward the season's end in some of the well-known snow holders like Zürs, Zermatt, Davos, Grindelwald, Cervinia, Alpe-d'Huez, Courchevel, Val d'Isère, Chamonix, and Les Diablerets near Gstaad. You must remember, though, that even in these late snowers good powder is usually limited to the higher parts of the mountain, and the higher parts usually are, alas, also the steeper.

I went to Grindelwald once in April, and although there was still good snow up at Kleine Scheidegg and on the Oberjoch, the runs were beyond my poor power to negotiate. As a result I spent most of my time on the lower runs skiing a new kind of crud formed of melting snow and the runoff from the mounds of manure that the farmers had collected all winter in anticipation of spring planting. But do you want to know something funny? I had a marvelous time skiing in Grindelwald, anyway. This either says something extremely negative about my psychological makeup or something extremely positive about the pleasures of skiing in general and Alpine skiing in particular. I prefer to think it's the latter.

Afterword
and Afterwarning

I feel I would be less than honest if I didn't own up to the existence of one tragic flaw in the sport of skiing. Skiing is addictive. Sometimes it gets hold of a person and won't let go, turning him into a hopeless skiaholic, making him sacrifice his life, his fortune, and his sacred honor to the snow gods.

There was, I remember, this brilliant and hard-working California girl who won scholarships all through college and then not only was admitted to the medical school of a major university but was given a full scholarship there. It also happened, according to the them-that-has-gets theory of life, that this girl was an excellent skier. She was so excellent, in fact, that one day when she was skiing, the ski school director tapped her on the shoulder and inquired if she'd be interested in teaching. Since the fall quarter at the university had just ended and she *could* take the winter quarter off, and, well, she *did* need the rest . . . the rapture of the heights got her. She kept postponing her return to school until she blew the scholarship. She's even reached the point now that she doesn't leave the resort in the summer, preferring to hang around doing menial maintenance chores, waiting for the first sight of flakes.

And this is not an isolated case. Just chat a bit with the kids fitting your boots and mounting your bindings in the ski shop. See how many sheepishly confess they went to college for a while in Colorado or Utah or Nevada but "majored in skiing" with the inevitable result.

Grown men, too, have been known to desert their families for the slopes. Sensible women, some from socially prominent families, have succumbed to skiing to the extent of divorcing their husbands and marrying ski instructors.

So if you suspect yourself of being a potential skiaholic, don't even take that first run. I don't want you on my conscience.

APPENDIX A

Mail Order Sources for Ski Clothing

ABERCROMBIE & FITCH
87-01 69th Ave.
Forest Hills, N.Y. 11375
   fog-resistant ski glasses
   coats (shearling, suede, sheep-
      skin)
   parkas
   gloves
   electric socks and mittens

ALASKA SLEEPING BAG COMPANY
13150 S.W. Dawson Way
Beaverton, Ore. 97005
   parkas (down, wolf, lamb)
   warm-up pants
   hats and hoods
   face protectors
   mittens and gloves
   sweaters (Cowichan, Iceland)
   socks
   snowmobile suits
   turtlenecks
   after-ski boots
   sunglasses
   coats (steerhide, New Zealand
      suede, shearling)
   Hudson's Bay jackets

ANTARTEX
120 Greenwich Ave.
Greenwich, Conn. 06830
   sheepskin and lambskin coats
   sheepskin-lined after-ski boots

AUSTRAL ENTERPRISES
P.O. Box 5033—Ballard Station
Seattle, Wash. 98107
   Aussie hats
   Australian wool yarn and
      sweater patterns

EDDIE BAUER
1737 Airport Way S.
Seattle, Wash. 98134
   parkas
   gloves
   mittens (down, fur, leather,
      wool)
   hats
   jackets (suede, leather, fur)
   after-ski boots
   socks
   underwear
   turtlenecks
   sweaters

L. L. BEAN, INC.
Freeport, Me. 04032
  hats
  parkas
  gloves and mittens
  underwear
  chamois face masks
  warm-up pants
  turtlenecks
  sweaters
  after-ski boots
  socks
  sheepskin innersoles
  sheepskin rugs

BERMAN BUCKSKIN CO.
26 Hennepin Ave.
Minneapolis, Minn. 55401
  suede jackets
  buckskin boots
  mittens and gloves
  hats (leather, fur)
  snowmobile suits

DEERSKIN TRADING POST
Rt. 1 at 114
Danvers, Mass. 01923
  lambskin and sheepskin coats
  after-ski boots
  parkas
  turtlenecks
  gloves
  underwear
  electric socks and mittens
  hats
  snowmobile suits
  warm-up pants

GERRY
P.O. Box 5544
Denver, Colo. 80217
  mittens
  net underwear
  socks

HUSFLIDEN
Postboks 19
Trondheim, Norway
  hand-knit Norwegian sweaters
  and hats

KLØVER HUSET
Strandgaten 13
5001 Bergen, Norway
  hand-knit Norwegian sweaters
  and hats
  sealskin boots
  after-ski jerkins
  reindeer fells

D. MACGILLIVRAY & CO.
Muir of Aird, Benbecula
Outer Hebrides, Scotland
  sweaters (fisherman's knit,
  Aran wool)
  hand-knitted Harris wool socks
  knitting wool

THE ORVIS COMPANY, INC.
Manchester, Vt. 05254
  underwear
  parkas
  socks
  gloves
  sweaters (Australian water-
  proof, fisherman's)
  sunglasses
  electric socks

OUTDOOR WORLD
P.O. Box 1880
Estes Park, Colo. 80517
  after-ski boots
  lederhosen
  turtlenecks
  socks

P & S Sales
P.O. Box 155
Tulsa, Okla. 74102
  (men's wear only; Government
    surplus)
  parkas
  underwear
  hats
  face masks
  goggles

RefrigiWear
71 Inip Dr.
Inwood, Long Island, N.Y. 11696
  hats and hoods
  socks
  face protectors

Shannon International
Airport
Ireland
  turtlenecks
  fisherman's knit sweaters

The Swiss Cheese Shop
Box 429
Monroe, Wisc. 53566
  Tyrolean hats
  lederhosen

The Talbots
222 North St.
Hingham, Mass. 02043
  turtlenecks
  children's parkas

Norm Thompson
1805 N.W. Thurman St.
Portland, Ore. 97209
  hats
  parkas
  sweaters (Everest, Cowichan)
  gloves and mittens
  socks
  underwear
  shearling coats
  turtlenecks

Uber Tanning Co. and
Uber Glove Co.
Owatonna, Minn. 55060
  gloves and mittens
  leather jackets

APPENDIX B
Guidebooks to Ski Resorts

American

Casewit, Curtis W., *United Air Lines Guide to Western Skiing.*
Garden City, N.Y., Doubleday, 1967.

Huggins, Robert and Eleanor, *Skiing in the West.* San Jose,
Calif., H. M. Goushá Co., 1967.

Rand, Abby, *Ski North America: Your Guide to the Top 28 Resorts.* Philadelphia, Pa., J. B. Lippincott, 1969.

European

De Linde, C. A., *Your Guide to Skiing Resorts.* London, Alvin
Redman, 1965.

Galin, Saul. *Skiing in Europe.* New York, Hawthorn Books, Inc.,
1967.

Le Guide de la Neige, 1969, 14th ed. Paris, Imprimerie Commer-
ciale, 1969.

Rand, Abby, *Ski Guide to Europe: The Fabulous Forty.* New
York, Award House, 1968.

Ronay, Egon, *Egon Ronay's AA Ski Europe.* London, Automobile Association, 1966.

International

Pan American (prepared by), *Ski New Horizons.* New York,
Simon and Schuster, 1969.

215

APPENDIX C
Guide to U.S. Run Markings

ail Marking Signs

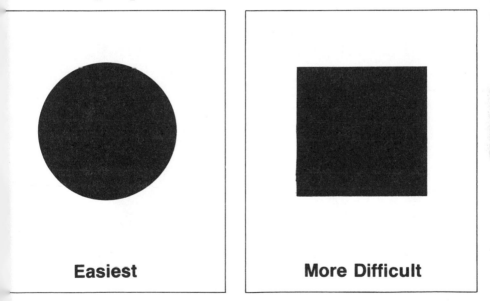

| Easiest | More Difficult |

Most Difficult

Caution

Closed

Emergency Telephone

APPENDIX D

National Skier's Courtesy Code

1. All skiers shall ski under control. Control shall mean in such a manner that a skier can avoid other skiers or objects.
2. When skiing downhill and overtaking another skier, the overtaking skier shall avoid the skier below him.
3. Skiers approaching each other on opposite traverses pass to the right.
4. Skiers shall not stop in a location that will obstruct a trail or stop where they are not visible from above or impede the normal passage of other skiers when loading or unloading.
5. A skier entering a trail or slope from a side or intersecting trail shall first check for approaching downhill skiers.
6. A standing skier shall check for approaching downhill skiers before starting.
7. When skiers are walking or climbing in a ski area, skis should be worn and the climber or walker shall keep to the side of the trail or slope.
8. All skiers shall wear safety straps or other devices to prevent runaway skis.
9. Skiers shall keep off closed trails and posted areas and shall observe all traffic signs and other regulations as prescribed by the ski area.

APPENDIX E

Sources for Ski and Travel Posters

Airlines

AIR FRANCE
638 Fifth Ave.
New York, N.Y. 10022

LUFTHANSA
410 Park Ave.
New York, N.Y. 10022

PAN AMERICAN
P.O. Box 1111
New York, N.Y. 10017

PANAGRA
Room 4427, Chrysler Bldg.
New York, N.Y. 10017

SAS
638 Fifth Ave.
New York, N.Y. 10020

SWISSAIR
Statler Office Bldg.
Room 700
20 Providence St.
Boston, Mass. 02116

Equipment Manufacturers

BECONTA, INC.
381 Park Ave. S.
New York, N.Y. 10016

DARTMOUTH SKIS, INC.
Hanover, N.H. 03755

HART SKI MANUFACTURING CO.
630 Pierce Butler Rt.
St. Paul, Minn. 55104

HEAD SKI COMPANY, INC.
Timonium, Md. 21093

NORTHLAND SKIS
2325 Endicott St.
St. Paul, Minn. 55114

SASKA SKI EQUIPMENT CO.
12436 Santa Monica Blvd.
Los Angeles, Cal. 90025

SPORT-OBERMEYER
Box 130, Aspen, Colo. 81611

WHITE STAG
5200 S.E. Harney Dr.
Portland, Ore. 97206

Tourist Offices

AUSTRIAN STATE TOURIST DEPT.
444 Madison Ave.
New York, N.Y. 10022

CANADIAN GOVERNMENT
TRAVEL BUREAU
150 Kent St.
Ottawa, Ontario, Canada

FRENCH GOVERNMENT
TOURIST OFFICE
610 Fifth Ave.
New York, N.Y. 10020

GERMAN TOURIST INFORMATION
OFFICE
500 Fifth Ave.
New York, N.Y. 10036

ITALIAN STATE TOURIST OFFICE
626 Fifth Ave.
New York, N.Y. 10020

MINISTERE DU TOURISME
PROVINCE DE QUEBEC
12 Rue Saint-Anne
Quebec, Canada

NORWEGIAN NATIONAL
TRAVEL OFFICE
290 Madison Ave.
New York, N.Y. 10017

OFFICIAL INQUIRY & TOURIST
OFFICES, AUSTRIA
Kitzbühel, Tyrol, Austria
St. Anton, Tyrol, Austria
Verkehrsverein, Tyrol, Austria

OFFICIAL INQUIRY & TOURIST
OFFICE, SWITZERLAND
Adelboden, Switzerland
Arosa, Switzerland
Berner Oberland, Switzerland
Davos, Switzerland
Grindelwald, Switzerland
Gstaad, Switzerland
Klosters, Switzerland
St. Moritz, Switzerland
Wengen, Switzerland
Zermatt, Switzerland

SWISS NATIONAL TOURIST OFFICE
608 Fifth Ave.
New York, N.Y. 10020

This list is courtesy of Aerial Tramway—Cannon Mountain Ski Area, Franconia Notch State Park, Franconia, N.H.

APPENDIX F

Regional Divisions
United States Ski Association

ROSS BUILDING, SUITE 300
1726 CHAMPA ST.
DENVER, COLORADO 80202

United States Eastern Amateur Ski Association, 20 Main St., Littleton, N.H. 03561, with jurisdiction over New England, New York, New Jersey, Pennsylvania, Delaware, Maryland, District of Columbia, Virginia, West Virginia, North Carolina, South Carolina, Georgia and Florida.

Alaska Division, P.O. Box 3-3923, Anchorage, Alaska 99502, with jurisdiction over the State of Alaska.

Central Division, 118 S. Union Street, Traverse City, Mich. 49684, with jurisdiction over Ohio, Michigan, Indiana, Illinois, Wisconsin, Minnesota, Iowa, North Dakota, South Dakota east of the Missouri River, Missouri, except the counties of Jackson and Clay, Kentucky, Tennessee, Arkansas, Louisiana, Mississippi and Alabama.

Northern Division, 3707 Augusta, Butte, Mont. 59701, with jurisdiction over the State of Montana, Yellowstone National Park, and in Northern Wyoming the counties of Park, Hot Springs, Bighorn, Washakie, Sheridan, Johnson, Campbell, Crook, Weston, Natrona and Converse.

Rocky Mountain Division, 214 Equitable Building, Denver, Colo. 80202, with jurisdiction over the States of Colorado, New Mexico, Nebraska, Kansas, Oklahoma, Texas, the counties of Niobrara, Carbon, Albany, Platte, Goshen, and Laramie in Southern Wyoming, South Dakota west of the Missouri River, and the counties of Jackson and Clay in the State of Missouri.

Intermountain Division, 3584 S.W. Temple, Salt Lake City, Utah 84115, with jurisdiction over the State of Utah, and over the counties of Teton, Sublette, Lincoln, Sweetwater and Uinta in Wyoming: and over the following counties in Southeastern Idaho: Bannock, Bearl Lake, Bonneville, Blaine, Butte, Camas, Caribou, Cassia, Clark, Custer, Franklin, Freemont, Gooding, Jefferson, Jerome, Lemhi, Lincoln, Madison, Mindoka, Oneida, Power, Teton, Twin Falls, and the counties of Elko, Eureka and White Pine in Nevada.

Far West Ski Association, 812 Howard St., San Francisco, Calif. 94103, with jurisdiction over the States of California, Arizona and Hawaii, and the State of Nevada with the exception of the counties of Elko, Eureka and White Pine.

Pacific Northwest Division, Box 434, Yakima, Wash. 98901, with jurisdiction over the States of Washington, Oregon and over the following counties in the State of Idaho: Ada, Adams, Benewah, Boise, Bonner, Boundary, Canyon, Clearwater, Elmore, Gem, Idaho, Kootenai, Latah, Lewis, Nez Perce, Owyhee, Payette, Shoshone, Valley and Washington.